ULTRALIGHT BIKE TOURING
AND BIKEPACKING

ULTRALIGHT BIKE TOURING AND BIKEPACKING

The Ultimate Guide to Lightweight Cycling Adventures

JUSTIN LICHTER AND JUSTIN KLINE

FALCONGUIDES

GUILFORD, CONNECTICUT
HELENA, MONTANA

FALCONGUIDES®

An imprint of Rowman & Littlefield
Falcon and FalconGuides are registered trademarks and Make Adventure Your Story is a trademark of Rowman & Littlefield.

Distributed by NATIONAL BOOK NETWORK

Copyright © 2017 Rowman & Littlefield

Cover photo and all photos within the book by Beth Puliti (www.beth puliti.com) unless otherwise noted.

British Library Cataloguing-in-Publication Information available

Library of Congress Cataloging-in-Publication Data available
ISBN 978-1-4930-2397-4 (paperback)
ISBN 978-1-4930-2398-1 (e-book)

♾™ The paper used in this publication meets the minimum requirements of American National Standard for Information Sciences—Permanence of Paper for Printed Library Materials, ANSI/NISO Z39.48-1992.

You haven't lived until you've lived with only what you can carry under your own power.

CONTENTS

Prelude viii

1. Bikepacking History and Principles 1

2. Trip Planning Considerations. 13

3. Bikepacking Carrying Methods
   and Setups 31

4. Backcountry Skills and Gear. 53

5. Dealing with Trailside Troubles 106

6. Bikepacking for Speed
   and Endurance .118

7. A Few of Our Favorites:
   Destinations and Setups. 131

Index. 157

About the Authors 164

PRELUDE

I lift the small ceramic saucer to my lips, capturing every bit of warmth possible with my exposed fingertips. It's some of the best-tasting chai I've had in some time, perhaps ever, and I'm not in the local coffee shop, boutique teahouse, or an upscale restaurant. I'm sitting cross-legged, wearing Russian galoshes and most of the clothing I own at the moment, on the plywood floor of a railcar-turned-home high in the Tien Shan Mountains of Kyrgyzstan. Just 30 minutes earlier, my wife and I were slowly turning the pedals over as we made our way up a seemingly endless climb, dodging mud bogs, rolling through deep ruts, and crossing countless streams. The forward progress of our incredible adventure had just come to a halt though, as a leather-faced local man vehemently signaled us from a distance. With slight hesitation, we laid the bikes aside and made our way over a mid-calf-deep brook toward the gentleman.

Like most other people we encountered in the country, he spoke no English so it was a game of Charades, only our one-word clues were dictated in Kyrgyz and Russian. Fortunately, hand gestures and visual cues can be universal throughout the world, and we quickly learned that our dwindling mountain path was soon to be impassable as it was blocked by snow taller than us. We knew this was a distinct possibility when we plotted and began the route in early spring, but it didn't prepare us for reaching the actual conclusion of defeat.

Despite sharing little more than a single common word in our vocabularies, the man clearly read the dejected looks on our faces as we struggled to process turning around and forging a new route or spending days attempting to cross a high alpine snowfield in frigid temperatures with insufficient rations for the added duration. That was the moment he uttered the Russian word *chay*, or tea. With our other options certainly less appealing, a warm drink and temporary shelter from the relentless elements seemed like an obvious solution.

While he gathered wood and animal dung to heat the tea, we entered his home, a hunter green caravan, the only man-made structure amid the barren landscape. Despite being on wagon wheels, this small structure looked like it hadn't moved in decades. Within the cozy confines, we were surrounded by the most basic of provisions: meat hanging from the ceiling to cure, a bucket of water from the nearby stream glazed over with ice, and chickens jostling around the steel stove as its heat began to radiate.

The small, knee-high table quickly become a buffet of everything this stranger had to offer—tea, sugar, butter, naan, cookies, and wrapped candies. We reciprocated by offering our own biscuits, peanut butter, and a number of other ready-to-eat snacks we'd been carrying. With some finagling of a makeshift antenna, our host tuned in some background music on his battery-powered radio, the

sole source of electronic entertainment in his off-grid home-stead. Carrying on any sort of conversation was impossible, but the smiles, gestures, and politeness made it clear that we were all enjoying each other's company over the most basic of meals.

After the last drops of tea were poured and the final crumbs of stale cookies were consumed, it was time to move on. We had a significant amount of descending to do before dark so we could make camp at a low enough elevation to stay warm overnight and position ourselves to resume an alternate alpine route the next morning. What had felt like a disappointing misadventure at first turned into an unforgettable encounter and temporary bond between strangers from very distant lands. We parted ways with a warm feeling inside that took more than tea to elicit. We had reached a part of the world that saw little, if any, bicycle travelers, and this was just the beginning of our life-changing adventures to come.

This journey would have been impossible with a traditional touring setup and fully loaded bicycle. With a precise kit and capable off-road setup, we were able to explore a rugged and remote part of the world we had only dreamed of, and meet people who lived unimaginably different lives. The days and months that followed were some of the most memorable we've ever had on a bicycle. This was expedition touring at its finest, and like most great adventures it did not come without challenges.

Traveling light by bike walks a fine line between being prepared and relying on your surroundings—allowing you to cycle farther, faster, and truly enjoy the riding experience. With only the essentials, you're able to engage with your surroundings, and that is when travel and adventure by bike is at its best.

—Justin Kline

The pages that follow strive to inspire, instruct, and instill the necessities for unforgettable ultralight overnight adventures by bike.

1.
BIKEPACKING HISTORY AND PRINCIPLES

Some of the earliest adventures by bicycle date back to the late 1800s when intrepid Europeans would take their high horse and penny farthing far beyond the normal recreational ride. Not long after, the invention of the Rover (or Safety Cycle) created the form-factor for the bicycle we know and love today. The Rover was a catalyst for lightweight touring and yet-to-be-dubbed "bikepacking" adventures. Without panniers and modern-day gear, and with limited development of carrying systems, early-day bicycle travelers were forced to carry only the necessities for self-supported exploration.

Although likely not by choice, the US 25th Infantry of the late nineteenth century set an early precedent for lightweight bicycle exploration in America. Also known as the Buffalo Soldiers, the brigade of roughly twenty-four African Americans, led by Lieutenant James A. Moss, undertook a number of bicycle expeditions, including a 1,900-mile journey from Missoula, Montana, to St. Louis, Missouri, in forty days (including six rest/repair days). Although their turn-of-the-century bicycles and gear were far from light, the rudimentary carrying systems available and the pressure to proceed faster than foot soldiers and cavalry ultimately forced the Buffalo Soldiers to employ a minimalist philosophy from the get-go.

Each soldier was equipped with a handlebar roll that included his tent, a set of underwear, two pairs of socks, a handkerchief, and a toothbrush and powder. Within the main triangle of the bike, they carried dense rations primarily made up of bread, bacon, beans, canned beef, coffee, and sugar. Less-essential cargo, such as a towel, soap, and cloth for wiping down the bikes, was carried by every other soldier and shared, while medicine, tools, spare parts, and matches were further dispersed among squad leaders and those managing relevant duties. In total, the weight of each loaded bike was about 55 to 59 pounds, excluding the 10-pound rifle and fifty-round cartridge belt. Despite the evolution of the bicycle, camping gear, and carrying systems over the last century, a majority of today's long-distance touring cyclists still carry a similar average weight, if not more.

On the lighter side of things, the recent evolution of self-supported endurance races like the 2,745-mile Tour Divide challenge has helped shape and redefine what's possible for lightweight independent travel by bike. These days the term *ultralight* has taken on new meaning and spawned the latest segment in bike touring: bikepacking. Effectively a hybrid between ultralight backpacking and bike touring, bikepacking focuses on predominantly off-road overnight cycling trips with a lightweight and concise kit to maximize riding enjoyment and exploration possibilities while minimizing the impact on bike handling.

As camping gear and technical apparel have evolved to be lighter, more durable, and more compact, the overall carrying volume for an overnight kit has reduced drastically. This means that in many touring scenarios, panniers and even racks are no longer necessary. While carbon fiber may not be the new steel for epic adventures abroad, frame bags can in fact be the new panniers for many bicycle journeys, even those spanning weeks, months, or years.

Our motivations may vary, but there is no denying the enjoyment that comes with traveling self-sufficiently by bike. The acquisition of possessions and surrounding ourselves with them is an unfortunate development in today's

A fully functioning lightweight bikepacking setup, complete with digital SLR carrying capabilities, ready to tackle a variety of terrain.

society. Genuine experiences are enhanced when you simplify things. The same holds true when traveling by bike. It takes only a few simple considerations to get the most out of overnight bike adventures:

- Carry only what you need.

- Maximize your riding experience.

- Travel farther.

CARRY ONLY WHAT YOU NEED

It may sound simple in theory, but we all have the inclination to carry more possessions than we actually need. We'll throw in the second pair of underwear because "it doesn't take up that much extra room," the spare fuel canister "in case the first one runs out," the inflatable pillow because "it will be more comfortable to sleep with," the second pair of gloves "in case the first gets wet." The list is seemingly endless, and we can always find a way to justify the extra items. Well, except perhaps a campstool. If you are committed to sleeping on the ground, you might as well enjoy sitting on it as well, right? Don't overthink (and overpack) beyond what you actually need. Each one of those "it's not that heavy" and "what-if" items eventually adds up to weigh you down.

Perhaps the most rewarding component of traveling with only the necessities is ultimately how it shapes your journey. With your most basic needs fulfilled, the "what-if" items become replaced (and resolved) by what your immediate and ever-changing surroundings have to offer. When

While traveling through remote stretches of the Himalayas, shelter took on a variety of forms, including this third-grade classroom. Improvising allowed us to have a more intimate experience with the local community, and in this case form lasting friendships.

exploring a new place and undertaking a foreign adventure, the people and opportunities you encounter provide a far richer experience than attempting to travel in a self-contained bubble seeking to resolve every "what-if" scenario. The reality is that what you may have left behind can likely be found, jerry-rigged, or substituted at some point along, or not far off, your intended route.

Fortunately, by the nature of their design, a frame bag–based carrying system offers limited carrying volume compared to its pannier-based predecessor. For those accustomed to overpacking, the significant volume reduction may initially seem challenging, but ultimately it

Vice Versa

Wild camping in Kyrgyzstan is best enjoyed with a sampling of the local flavor. Just don't forget a chaser.

We all have our vices, and what better time to indulge than when escaping the daily grind and traveling by bike? The goal of ultralight bike touring is to leave behind the unnecessary items, not to unnecessarily remove the fun from the journey. There is always a nook or cranny to fit a flask, chocolate bar, or tallboy(s) of microbrew so it's ready to be revealed after a long day in the saddle.

provides the framework and guidance to truly pare down your kit to the actual necessities.

The key is finding your sweet spot, and with experience it moves farther down the weight curve than you might think. But don't worry, nobody will make you cut your toothbrush handle off or count your squares of TP.

MAXIMIZE YOUR RIDING EXPERIENCE

Flowing singletrack, pitched just right to create a natural downhill-trending pump track on an aspen-lined mountainside, occasionally opening up to endless vistas, with your legs light, fresh, and eager to rip around the next bend in hopes that it's never-ending—it's what mountain biking dreams are made of.

Now imagine the scenario except with an unevenly weighted load protruding beyond the width of the trail, the sound of dust kicking up behind you replaced by rattling of the rigid contact points between rack and panniers. Suddenly, around each bend you're hoping the trail becomes tamer, with an end in sight to rest your weary legs.

A mountain biking dream, but one of us is able to enjoy it more due to the difference in packing methods and weight distribution.

High alpine singletrack is best enjoyed with a light load, particularly in the Swiss Alps.

It's not just about the additional effort it takes to lug around added weight on your bike. A minimalistic setup distributed properly on your bike (see chapter 3) makes a noticeable difference in your bike's handling quality, particularly off-road. With a properly balanced lightweight load, your bike can be nearly as nimble as when unloaded, ultimately maximizing your riding experience while delivering you to a new destination at the end of the day.

It's often said that the journey is the destination, and there is no scenario more applicable to this than a bikepacking or bike touring adventure. The sights, the sounds, the suffering—all form unforgettable memories when exploring by bike. When you dial down your kit and minimize the heavy-pedal suffering, you make the journey that much more enjoyable.

TRAVEL FARTHER

A compact kit leads to a lighter steed, which ultimately allows you to travel farther. The beauty in that means different things to different people: covering more miles in a day, knocking off short distances with ease and leaving more off-the-bike time to enjoy, or traveling to rugged and remote areas otherwise unreachable by fully loaded touring bikes.

While it's hard to fathom ticking off 200-plus off-road miles in a day like the bikepacking legends do regularly on the Great Divide Trail, it is inspirational and a testament to what is possible when traveling light. A lightweight overnight kit can make 20 miles, 50 miles, or even a century feel far more feasible. As the distances come easier, the

Exploring hidden bunkers on the border of Afghanistan.
JUSTIN KLINE

When Ultralight Just Ain't Right

The rugged mountainous routes in Nepal are prime territory for large-volume tires and big wheels like 27.5 and 29 inchers.

There are plenty of places to save weight when it comes to both your bike and gear, but you should carefully consider the terrain you plan to undertake before counting grams and shelling out dollars. While it's tempting to focus on rotational weight savings, skimping on tire size and volume in favor of weight can leave you with bone-jarring results. Rugged terrain demands traction, control, stability, and comfort, particularly when riding a rigid bike with added cargo. The merits of plus-size tires and larger-diameter wheels should not be discounted when traveling off-road.

only decision you're left with is whether to ride farther, finish the day earlier, or explore more.

It may seem like an afterthought, but when traveling to rugged and remote locations, a compact, lightweight setup is nearly as important when you're not pedaling as when you are. Pushing up steep hiking trails and animal paths, organizing transportation or finding an exit strategy when plans A and B do not pan out, fording rivers, boarding trains, are best undertaken with a lightweight setup. None of these scenarios may be in the trip itinerary, but they're bound to happen when you pedal off the beaten path, and it's these moments when you are unable to pedal that remind us why light is right.

Boarding international trains . . .

Loading onto bus roofs . . .

Pushing above 16,000 feet . . .

Whether pedaling, pushing, carrying, or transporting your bike, a lighter load makes the journey more enjoyable and opens up possibilities for more adventures.

2.
TRIP PLANNING CONSIDERATIONS

Planning your first, or next, overnight outing can (and should) be nearly as fun as the trip itself. Dreaming up ideas and then laying out a topo map or endlessly scouring Google Maps to plot a course is when it all begins. Whether you're following an established route or blazing uncharted territory to connect two dots, you're cranking up the stoke meter for exploration. From there the anticipation for adventure only builds as you sort through gear and gather the necessities.

Short bikepacking trips can be arranged spontaneously with little planning, so this step should never be an inhibiting factor in taking a trip. When you are looking to go light, though, the planning stage makes all the difference. It's when you know what to expect that you can eliminate all the "what-if" items that bog so many people down. With some basic knowledge of your route, weather, and riding partners, the foundation is laid for a lightweight adventure. Proper planning before your departure allows

You never know where you might have the opportunity to sleep when traveling by bike.

you to hit the road or trail on the proper bike with sufficient clothing, adequate gear, and nothing more.

While the best adventures are often left to chance and follow a course that may never have been plotted, starting with a basic understanding of your intended route creates the framework for what bike to ride and what to bring or, equally as important: what to leave behind. A camp stove, for instance, can be a necessity in Central Asia where food sources are scant, but might be best left behind in Southeast Asia where inexpensive prepared food can be located in even the smallest of villages.

Fortunately, there are seemingly unending resources for route planning and future trip inspiration. Outside of following someone's previous itinerary, there is no golden ticket for assembling a route, but using several of the following resources opens up numerous possibilities for overnight adventures: Google Maps, DeLorme Gazetteers by state, Maps.me, Strava, Map My Ride, Adventure Cycling Association, bikeovernights.com, bikepacking.com, bikepacking.net, ridebygps.com, GPS trax, Garmin Connect, topofusion.com, caltopo.com, National Geographic mapping software, and Scribble Maps.

The miles come easy when the terrain is flat and hard packed, like during the dry season in Vietnam.
JUSTIN KLINE

In the mountains, every mile is earned and rarely comes without added effort.

When setting the course for your journey, evaluate the terrain and never underestimate elevation gain. In the flatlands of Southeast Asia, knocking off 100K and being beachside by midafternoon may not be a problem, but trying to squeak out 50K off-road in the rugged and demanding environment of the Rockies, Dolomites, Alps, or Himalayas is another story.

Once a route is in order, it's time to make sure your steed is up to the task, though as even the most tight-lipped and competitive of racers, Lance Armstrong, will admit, "It's not about the bike." Sure, one of the big advantages of traveling light is the ability to travel on a lighter bike with traditional gearing, but we're firm believers on rolling with what you have. If you're stocked with a quiver of bikes from which to choose the ideal bike for the job, great, but that should never inhibit an overnight bike excursion. Many of the best adventures begin with the bike that's already in your garage and the gear waiting to be used in your attic. Almost any bike is a capable vehicle for an adventure as long as you are willing to power it. Matching

Lighter Loads Allow for a Lighter Bike

A lightweight bikepacking setup that tackled the remote reaches of Central Asia. Russian galoshes were added for the common snow and river crossings.

With a compact kit even long-distance touring trips are no longer limited to overbuilt task-built bikes. Central Asia may be the last place you'd expect to see a sub-23-pound full-suspension carbon fiber World Cup XC race bike, but with minimal added gear weight and maximum interest in riding off-pavement, why not?

the bike for the terrain makes the pedaling a bit easier, but leaving the supposed boundaries of what your bike was designed for often leads to the most memorable journeys. Pavement, gravel, mixed surfaces, jeep trails, singletrack, snowmobile trails . . . all gateways to adventure.

One of the primary advantages of some basic route research is developing knowledge for what resources may or may not be available along the way. At 2.2 pounds per liter, water is likely to be one of the heaviest components of your kit, so finding reliable beta for water sources on your intended route can be a notable weight saver. Convenience stores, public restroom facilities, ponds, streams, and rivers are all viable refilling options along the way, especially when you are traveling with a SteriPEN or other water treatment option. The amount of water you start with will of course vary by ride duration, ability to resupply along the way, and if you'll be cooking at your destination.

Options for resupplying take on many different forms and may be more accessible than you think, even in rural developing countries.

Like water, food is another integral element to the kit that is relatively heavy, but typically convenient to resupply en route, making it an easy area to shed some pounds and volume without sacrificing comfort along the way. Restock at grocery stores, bakeries, convenience stores, and other local markets/roadside stands. Eating a meal at a restaurant along the way can decrease the amount of food you need to carry, provide a much-needed rest, and even afford you leftovers for the road. With a basic gauge of how much ground you'll be covering daily and accessibility to nourishment along the way, you can start with just a small food stash to get you going and a bit of reserves for the times when that next town isn't coming as soon as you expected. It's also enticing—and rewarding—to embrace the cuisine that's available along the way, whether that means foraging for greens or chowing down on burritos from the local eatery. A commitment not to cook breakfast and dinner and go stoveless (see chapter 4) can be another notable volume reducer as well.

Knowing the anticipated weather for your journey is another key planning area that allows you to shed weight before turning the first pedal stroke. It's easy enough to pack a wardrobe capable of enduring a variety of weather, but gaining a better understanding of the climate, weather forecast, and elevation variances on your intended route can significantly reduce your clothing load. Outside of the short-range forecast, be sure to take into account the primary weather characteristics of the route: rain/monsoon season, snowfall, elevation, sun exposure, high alpine thunderstorms, and so on. Despite what most people think,

High alpine routes typically require supplemental layers to maintain warmth overnight, for early morning starts, and during seemingly never-ending descents.

the length of your journey should have little impact on the amount of clothing you bring along. Whether you're traveling by bike for two days, two weeks, or two years, there is little need to add or duplicate items in your wardrobe based on duration.

Planning the route will also dictate what shelter is necessary for the journey. Depending upon the distance between outposts of civilization, you may have the option to forgo bringing along an overnight kit altogether and rely on arranged lodging, such as hotels, guesthouses, backcountry huts, lean-tos, unoccupied shelters, or hosted lodging such as Couchsurfing and Warmshowers. The latter can be a great way to meet new like-minded people while traveling light, but don't let the temptation of a two-star

Existing shelters, even primitive ones, found along your route can provide respite from the weather and enable you to travel light.

hotel deter you from staying in the 1,000-star hotel: camping under the open sky.

Once you have an idea of the accessibility of water, food, and shelter along the route, take into account if this will be a solo journey or if you'll be riding with others. An overnight outing with riding partners not only provides the opportunity to have an incredible experience together, but it also allows you to disperse the weight of non-personal items. While food, water, and clothing remain as fairly fixed individual items, sharing the necessities for shelter, cooking, bike repair, and first aid are easily divided among two or more riders. Some of the best items to disperse and avoid redundancy between trip-mates are tents, stoves, cooking pots, repair kits (including pump and Allen keys/multi-tool), and first-aid kits. Traveling couples or small

Dispersing non-personal gear accordingly is also an ideal way to even the riding pace when there is a disparity in fitness and/or riding ability within the group. The noticeable difference in these two loads proved to set the perfect pace in Central Asia.

familes may find it warmer, lighter, and more comfortable to sleep beneath a single down camping quilt, such as the Enlightened Equipment Accomplice, instead of in separate sleeping bags.

Some places, such as the United States, Canada, and some European countries, allow you to mail yourself supplies and food ahead of time. In the United States you can mail things to a post office by General Delivery. In Canada this is called Post Restante. The post offices will typically hold the mail for you for up to thirty days. Address the box as follows:

> Your name
> General Delivery
> Town, State, and Zip Code
> Estimated ETA: XX/XX/XXXX

This can help you save weight in your carry kit because you are able to access certain items at regular intervals. For example, you can send maps for future sections ahead and pick them up later or bump that heavier down jacket up for when your route goes higher in elevation.

Also, keep in mind that in the United States, if you mail your package priority with the USPS and don't open it, you can then forward it somewhere else for free.

INTERNATIONAL CONSIDERATIONS

While most lightweight adventures can be prepared for with little notice, international and long-term trips can require a bit of longer-range planning. Here's an overview to help with planning and scheduling timelines for long-distance adventures in foreign destinations:

Gantt Chart for Organization of Trip Planning

Activity	Duration	3–6 Months Before	2 Months Before	1 Month Before	2 Weeks Before	Final Details
Permits						
• Trekking/Backcountry Agencies	+/- 2 months					
• Fees	+/- 1 month					
• Park Fees	+/- 1 month					
Visas						
• Multiple/Single Entry Specifics	3–6 months					
• Deadlines	3–6 months					
• Fees	3–6 months					
• Applications	3–6 months					
• Applying for Passport	6 months					
Travel						
• Flights	3–6 months					
• Gear Drops	2 weeks					
• To/From Resupply	2 weeks					
• International Relations/Cultural Customs Research*	+/- 1 month					

Route Details						
• Restricted Areas	+/- 1 month					
• Resupply Options and Distances Between	+/- 2 months					
• Maps	+/- 2 months					
• Weather / Temps	+/- 2 months					
• Conditions / Terrain	+/- 2 months					
• Water Details	+/- 1 month					
On-Trail Logistics						
• Charging Electronics	2 weeks					
• Money, Exchange, Amount	2 weeks					
• Language	2 weeks					
• Communication, E-mail	2 weeks					
• Food: What are we eating? How?	2 weeks					
• Acclimatizing	2 weeks					
• Extra Passport Photos	2 weeks					
• Meds to Carry	2 weeks					
• Flora / Fauna Considerations	2 weeks					

Gantt Chart for Organization of Trip Planning (continued)

Activity	Duration	3–6 Months Before	2 Months Before	1 Month Before	2 Weeks Before	Final Details
Getting Gear or Obtaining Sponsorship						
• Bike Gear	+/- 1 month			■	■	■
• Pack	+/- 2 months		■	■	■	■
• Shelter	+/- 2 months		■	■	■	■
• Apparel	+/- 1 month			■	■	■
• Cooking	+/- 1 month			■	■	■
• Water Treatment	+/- 1 month			■	■	■
• Toiletries	+/- 1 month			■	■	■
• Sat Phone?	+/- 2 months		■	■	■	■
• Money / Grants	3–6 months	■	■	■	■	■
• Food	+/- 2 months			■	■	

Pre-Trip						
• Vaccines	3–6 months					
• Travel Insurance	2 weeks					
• Contacts for Advice	3–6 months					
• Training	+/- 2 months					
• Schedule for Planning	3–6 months					
• Political Climate	3–6 months					
• Blog, Website, Communications, etc.	+/- 2 months					
• Prescriptions for Meds	+/- 1 month					

JUSTIN LICHTER

PLAN YOUR OWN BACKYARD ADVENTURE

Don't have an extended period of time to take off on a bike tour? You don't need it to head out on a "S24O," a phrase coined by Rivendell Bicycle Works founder Grant Petersen, which means "sub-24 hour overnight." Even with the demands of a 9-to-5 job and spending time with family, a S24O allows you to go ride for a few hours, spend the night out, and return to your responsibilities the next morning. We caught up with Petersen to discuss the philosophy and how he plans for his own S24O cycling adventures.

Please provide an introduction to your S24O philosophy:

Just because I don't have time for a twelve-day trip doesn't mean I can't make time for twelve one-day trips. I started doing S24Os in 1995 when I was sick of not getting out to distant pretty places because work and family didn't leave room for it. There's open space all around me, and just because it's close to city lights (sometimes) doesn't mean it's not perfect for these.

Any advice for planning an overnighter on a whim?

Tens of millions of people all over the world "camp out" involuntarily every night in bad weather and in bad places without the right gear for it, so don't overthink your overnight.

Overthinking and overplanning will get you all wound up—you'll be ordering a piece of unessential gear from Amazon two nights before you go. Allow yourself to be underequipped, because the whole beauty of the S24O is its convenience and shortness. I've forgotten sleeping bags, tent poles, food, sleeping pad, warm clothing . . . it all works out, and the best way to learn what you want to take is to forget it sometime. I try to bring something to sleep *in* (sleeping bag), *on* (pad), and, if there's any doubt, weather protection (tent).

Something best left behind?

Nothing's not worth bringing at least once to try it out. The other side of the "it's only one night, so you can do without it" is "it's only one night, so you don't have to lug it along for a week." It's your S24O, so personalize it and become your own expert.

Petersen is the author of *Just Ride* and *Eat Bacon, Don't Jog.*

Looking to minimize the excuses that prevent you from taking more riding trips? Keep the core items of your bike-packing kit readily available for spur-of-the-moment trips.

So many places to explore, so little time . . .

Here is a 30-minute prep plan that can have you out the door within, well, 30 minutes.

- Keep the bike tuned so it's ready to roll on a moment's notice.

- Keep a small storage bin, shelf, or dedicated space for your kit.

- Repair items, first-aid kit, carrying system, shelter, headlamp, and sleeping pad can remain packed and ready to go for the next trip.

- When possible keep a set of clean clothing and outerwear ready to go with the kit as well.

- Sleeping bag (which should not be stored compressed), food, and water will be all you need to grab-and-go.

3.
BIKEPACKING CARRYING METHODS AND SETUPS

The foundation of ultralight touring and bikepacking starts with the carrying system. Racks, panniers, trailers, and backpacks all have their place for bicycle touring, but when you are looking to cover more ground, turn the pedals over more easily, and enjoy the simplicity and freedom of a compact

An international expedition kit for two on an open-ended journey, spread out and ready to load onto the bikes.

setup on your bike, then an ultralight/bikepacking configuration, utilizing only frame bags, is the way to go. Carrying less weight means you can cover more ground, have less fatigue on your body and bike, and enjoy a better-handling bike, which is especially important when exploring singletrack.

Frame bags are the ultimate lightweight carrying solution, and depending upon the bike, a typical setup can include a main triangle frame bag, oversize seat bag, and a large handlebar roll bag. By utilizing these types of bags that attach directly to your seatpost, frame, and handlebars, you will save significant weight before you even consider what to bring along.

Choose your bags based upon your volume requirements and mounting preference, and don't feel obligated to stick with the same setup for every trip. Each bag provides

Frame bags are designed to fit your bike like a glove and can be outfitted to even the smallest of frames.

stand-alone carrying capacity, so the setup can be altered based on the amount of gear in tow. While a main triangle frame bag will be sized according to your bike, handlebar roll bags and seat bags are offered in a variety of sizes.

Each type of bag offers a different volume and weight. When choosing what bags to utilize, keep in mind the volume-to-weight ratio in order to maximize your packing efficiency and minimize weight. Also consider how the packing systems will affect the handling of the bike. As you can see in the chart below, there are considerable differences in volume-to-weight ratios. The higher the volume-to-weight ratio, the better, since you "get" more volume for each incremental ounce of weight you are carrying.

Carrying System	Average Empty Weight	Volume	Weight
Seatpost bags	~16 ounces	6–16 liters	1 ounce
Frame bags	~9 ounces–16 ounces	~6–14 liters	0.7–0.875 ounce
Handlebar bags	~1.9 ounces for the stuff sack + ~10–14 ounces for the attachment system	Up to ~25 liters	1.56 ounces
Fork-mounted cages and bags	5.3 ounces per side for cage + 4.5 ounces for each bag	~4.5 liters each	0.46 ounce
Accessory bags (stem and top tube bags)	~2.5–4 ounces	~0.41–~1.15 liters	0.16–0.287 ounce

Committing to a lightweight carrying system will ensure you start your journey on the right weight-saving foot. Not only will a frame bag configuration save you significant weight in itself, but the nature of such a packing system saves ounces and pounds because you won't be tempted (or able) to overpack.

A complete bikepacking kit utilizing a frame bag, seat bag, handlebar bag, and accessory bags.

PACKING YOUR GEAR

It's frustrating to dig through everything for your lighter, headlamp, or spork and have to pack and repack your entire kit multiple times per day. This leads to less time you are able to ride and tick off miles, or less time you are able to kick back on a beautiful ridgeline or near an amazing lake.

Packing your bike is one of those things that you can do a million different ways. The phrase wasn't designed for gear organization, but it applies here: "location, location, location." Once you find a method that works well for you, continue to pack your gear in the same locations, which eventually makes it second nature. You'll find it becomes faster and more efficient to pack up in the morning, during breaks, and when setting up camp in the evening.

Pack with purpose by keeping the following in mind:

- Plan accordingly with an idea of what you will need throughout the day based on terrain, weather, nutrition, and water so appropriate items are accessible.

- Keep a versatile outer layer and gloves handy for taking a break, long descents, and sudden changes in the weather.

- Unless you're in a desert climate, it doesn't hurt to plan for rain by ensuring your kit is packed to be waterproof each morning. Rain gear can be left toward the opening and outside of dry bags, since you'll be donning it when the sky opens up. This eliminates unpacking and repacking during sudden storms.

- Keep the maps that you will need for the day handy, and those for upcoming sections in case you make good time or want to review the upcoming route during a break. The other ones you can bury so they don't get wet or in the way when you are flipping through the accessible maps.

- In the morning separate your rations. Keep the food and snacks that you will use throughout the day on top and pack dinner and food reserves deeper in your bags.

- Keep your spork (or spoon) and knife accessible for meals throughout the day.

- And lastly, keep your headlamp accessible. There's nothing worse than pushing to try to find a camp spot as it's getting dark and burning a few precious minutes of dusk to get your headlamp out.

What's in the Bags?

Frame bag: A frame bag makes use of seldom-used space within the main triangle of your bike. Due to the location it also helps to stabilize the load. Make sure to pack heavier items in this area. Frame bags are typically good for your repair kit, first-aid kit, toiletries, cooking kit, and food that can be consumed while riding. When you pack food inside the frame bag, you'll want to minimize packaging and seal items in sandwich bags when possible so that they nest better and sit tighter in the space. Boxed items or anything in a rigid container will create awkward and inefficient packing. If anything is protruding from the frame bag it can interfere with your pedaling since the bags are soft-sided.

Most frame bags are equipped with a main compartment that is best filled with dense, rarely used items, and

A medium-size frame bag packed with a spare parts kit, repair items, and a few tools for quick access.

a smaller compartment or side pocket that is ideal storage for a commonly required condensed tool kit that covers adjusting the bike and fixing a flat.

A main triangle frame bag covers your bottle cage mounts, so you can either create two small holes to mount cages within the bag (assuming your other contents are well organized) or store a hydration bladder within the frame bag and have the hose running out to your top tube for convenient access. Some frame bags only cover part of the triangle area and allow space to have water bottle mounts. Both are options depending on how much carrying capacity and volume you need, and what your preference is for carrying and drinking water while riding. Additional areas for carrying sufficient water are on the fork legs, the underside of the down tube, and, of course, on your back.

A medium-size frame bag configured for carrying water and a few key quick-access repair and water treatment items.

Keep in mind that most frame bags are designed to fit specific frames and models. If your bike is not on that list don't worry, there are a number of custom frame bag manufacturers, or you can search online for the geometry of bikes that have similar specs.

Handlebar bag: A bikepacking handlebar bag consists of a roll-style stuff sack that fastens directly to the handlebars or is equipped with a mounting bracket that supports a removable dry bag/stuff sack. A handlebar bag is the best place for bulky, but relatively lightweight items. Excessive weight on the handlebars will impede the handling of your bike. You also don't want to place anything on the handlebars where the load isn't packed tightly, because it may shift while in motion or on rough terrain. The handlebar bag is an excellent spot to pack and roll up your entire sleeping kit (shelter, sleeping bag, sleeping pad, and even groundsheet). This system works really well, as you know exactly where your sleep system is located and can pop it right off the bike at the end of the day to lay out and set up. It also makes it incredibly easy to waterproof your sleeping bag since you will be using a stuff sack for this system anyway. A dry sack should keep your sleeping bag from getting wet, or you can line a stuff sack with a trash bag to create a waterproof stuff sack. Just make sure to close up the top of the trash bag well! If you are using a tent and have tent poles, they are ideally fastened to the outside of the handlebar bag on the front or bottom, depending upon the model.

When sizing to purchase the right roll bag, bigger is not always better. Size appropriately for style of handlebars and volume requirements. Roll-style handlebar bags

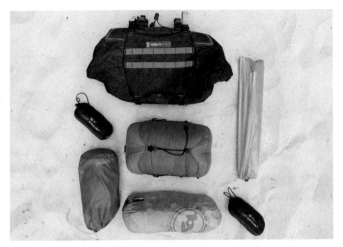

Flat bars enable you to utilize the full carrying capacity of a handlebar bag. Shown here is a sleeping kit for two and some additional clothing layers.

work well on straight bars, like on mountain bikes, since their capacity is not limited. With drop-style handlebars you will need to scale down the volume of the bag to fit within the confines of the drops and not interfere with the integrated brake/shifter levers. It's also worth considering alternative-style handlebars such as the Jones Loop H bar, since it not only provides additional hand positions but also additional mounting points for stabilizing the load.

When it comes to volume, keep in mind the larger you go the more you will sacrifice handling. Smaller-volume bags are better for singletrack, while larger bags can fit winter gear and bulkier loads, and will work on dirt roads, less technical terrain, and for long-distance touring. For front suspension bikes with a small frame and

Drop bars limit the carrying capacity of roll-style handlebar bags, but can still carry the majority of a sleep system, as shown here.

larger-diameter wheels, measure the clearance to ensure the handlebar bag won't scrape the front tire when the suspension is fully compressed.

Bikepacking handlebar bags are designed to integrate with your shifter and brake cables without interfering, by mounting either in front of or behind the cable routing. On drop bar–style bikes, and when cable length is limited, attempt to mount the handlebar bag in front of the cables without it pinching or altering the performance of braking and shifting. If you have the opportunity to run (or already have) longer cables, you can nestle the bag behind the cables, which ensures that shifting and braking performance is not compromised. Also consider the relative ease or difficulty each option presents, and whether you prefer to leave the bag mounted when packing/unpacking or completely remove the bag each time. A cradle-style mounting system, such as the Revelate Designs Harness, can be preferable if you are constantly removing the bag, so you don't have to fiddle with the cable routing each time.

For those who combine a passion for photography with bicycle travel, the handlebars are prime real estate for the camera. After all, the best shots are captured only when the camera is within reach. For convenient and secure access, consider a smaller square handlebar bag like the Ortlieb Ultimate 6 or an open-topped Porcelain Rocket DSLR Slinger to carry a bigger camera, lens, or other fragile electronics in an accessible spot.

A handlebar bag like the Ortlieb Ultimate 6 allows you easy access to your DSLR when riding. For off-road use consider a Revelate Designs Pocket or similar-style bag, packed with soft, rarely needed items like rain gear, to add carrying capacity and help stabilize the camera bag.

Seat Bag: The seat bag provides a streamlined way to carry items without using a rack, while still distributing some of the weight to the rear of the bike. It provides a single, easy-to-access, large-volume space that can house a variety of gear. Anything can go in here, ranging from spare clothes and cookware to cooking accessories and your shelter. Ideally this area is used for clothing and bulkier items, particularly those that need to be accessed throughout the day, since a seat bag provides relatively quick and easy access. Make sure to pack the contents securely and cinch the bag tight to your seat so it doesn't sway while riding. Typically, a fully loaded seat bag will need to be retightened to the seat rails as the contents compress, to

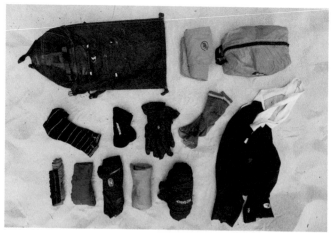

A bikepacking-style seat bag is best packed with dense and rarely needed items deeper inside, like this expedition-equipped repair kit, keeping the bulk of the weight closer to the bike itself. Lighter-weight and more commonly required items like clothing can then remain more accessible toward the opening.

ensure ideal handling. For day trips and shorter excursions, a seat bag can be used as a stand-alone carrying system. Some models have MOLLE (Modular Lightweight Load-carrying Equipment) loops so you can easily fasten other items on the outside as well.

Make sure the saddle rail bolts and seatpost bolts are securely tightened to prevent the seatpost from slipping due to the added weight of a loaded seat bag. On longer trips do some preventive maintenance by occasionally checking to ensure the seatpost has not slipped. It can be helpful to carry an additional bolt since continued slipping leads to overtightening, ultimately resulting in a stripped bolt.

Backpack: Cycling is best enjoyed with additional weight on the bike, not on the body, but when additional

A backpack like the Osprey Escapist can provide a quick and easy solution to adding volume and water-carrying capacity to a kit if necessary.

When traveling long-term by bike, the versatility of having a small backpack can allow you to reach some amazing places off the bike.

volume, water-carrying capacity, or laptop-carrying capabilities for long-distance travel are required, a backpack can be handy. There is no denying their convenience for drinking on the go, quickly accessing layers, and resupplying food without altering your bike bags. For long hike-a-bike routes a sturdy pack can also serve as a harness to attach your bike while carrying it up unridable pitches. If there are plans to incorporate off-the-bike adventures, you can also substitute a small backpack for one of the other carrying methods, depending on the trip.

Accessory Bags (Stem Bags and Top Tube Bags): If you need a little additional volume, there are a few small accessory bags that can add carrying capacity. These smaller accessory bags provide easy access to snacks, camera, arm warmers, and multi-tool and can eliminate the need for a backpack altogether. Some top tube bags tie in near the seatpost, while others attach near the head tube. The bag you use simply depends on preference and the shape of the items you are looking to stow. Stow bags can make things handy, but as shown in the chart at the beginning of this chapter, you don't receive much volume for the weight of each of these accessory pouches.

Fork leg–mounted cages like the Salsa Anything HD cages utilize an otherwise neglected area of the bike for carrying gear. This is an excellent location for carrying sleeping pads, cook sets, or an assortment of items when housed in a small dry bag. If your fork is not equipped with cage mounts, use hose clamps to mount them, but first wrap your fork legs with a section of old bike tube to preserve the paint and ensure the cages will not slip over time.

Fork-mounted carrying systems can be particularly helpful for adding carrying capacity to an otherwise underutilized portion of the bike. The Salsa Anything Cage and Anything Bags provide an off-the-shelf solution, although standard water bottle cages and lighter-weight stuff sacks can be fashioned with hose clamps and accessory straps. If added volume is required for a longer trip, fork-mounted cages and bags provide a better volume-to-weight ratio compared to other small accessory bag options.

Again, if you can, you are better off using the main packing systems (frame bag, seat bag, and handlebar bag and, if needed, backpack), which yield better volume-to-weight ratios.

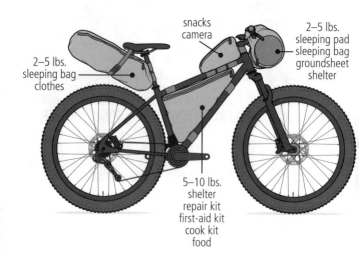

snacks
camera

2–5 lbs.
sleeping pad
sleeping bag
groundsheet
shelter

2–5 lbs.
sleeping bag
clothes

5–10 lbs.
shelter
repair kit
first-aid kit
cook kit
food

ROBERT L. PRINCE

Evolution of a Multiyear International Touring Setup

A proven lightweight kit is one that has evolved over time. With each journey, knowledge is gained and experiences occur that shape future adventures. One of the best ways to prepare for your next trip is to run through your last. What did you use? What could you have done without? What would have made the trip more enjoyable?

Over many years of pedaling on home and foreign soil, I learned what I craved, what I required, and, most important, what I could do without. The ability to explore off-road with limited weight was the end result and proves to be my ideal setup to this day. —Justin Kline

AN INTERVIEW WITH @ULTRAROMANCE

@ultraromance, or Benedict Wheeler to those of us closer to him, is known for his lifestyle as a purist bicycle traveler. He's graced the cover of *Bicycling* magazine, was interviewed by *UK Business Insider*, and is likely followed by you on Instagram. Benedict has the knack for traveling light, but without the Lycra, carbon, or flashy new components commonly associated with ultralight touring and bikepacking.

Here Benedict enlightens us about bicycle aesthetics, wheel size, and wardrobe:

Downtube shifters and metal baskets aren't typical elements on most people's modern-day touring setups. Tell us a little bit about your philosophy on touring without the latest tech.

Aesthetics are *very* important to me. The bicycle is my art, and I can't ride something that I don't think looks cool—it would be like Beyoncé carrying a TJ Maxx handbag. Unconscionable. For me, right now, old stuff looks better and oftentimes just works better too. Also, one of my favorite aspects of cycling is hacking old parts to work with what I deem a worthwhile, innovative modern upgrade. Eleven-speed 1x drivetrains for example. If you haven't tried 11-speed friction yet, you're living in 2015! It's simple, elegant, and won't fail on you in a bad crash out in the wilds or your backyard. Same goes for hydro disc brakes. I love discs, but for touring there is no reason to go beyond cable-actuated varieties. They work great and aren't gonna strand you out in the sticks with a hemorrhaged hydro

hose. I've seen it happen. Tech sells bikes and is good for the industry, but making things simpler, more intuitive, and aesthetically pleasing is better for everyone. Some people like the techy stuff with loads of suspension, but for me the bicycle is the pinnacle of human achievement due in part to its enduring simplicity in functionality. Add all the modern stuff, and you might as well just spend the extra $100 and get a motorcycle. But that's just me.

Bikes are available with batteries and motors nowadays. Any advice for someone looking to assemble a sturdy, simple, and reliable retro steed?

The best touring bikes have already been made. They existed from the early 1980s to mid-1990s in the form of steel-lugged and TIG-welded traditional geometry mountain bikes. They can be found on eBay and Craigslist for a fraction of what you'd pay for a new bike, plus they have the character and nostalgia that can't be bought in a modern bike shop. Twenty-six-inch wheels are strong, and the tires/tubes can be found throughout the undeveloped world. The frames are attractive, US or Japanese made, and often feature better tubing than anything modern. A tip would be to buy the biggest size you can possibly straddle. This will make it fit like a touring bike (fistful of post) and get the handlebars up nice and high.

You often travel in little more than cutoff shorts, but not everyone can pull off such a look. Any other tips for keeping a compact wardrobe while traveling by bike?

My everyday clothes are also my riding clothes. I'm also not really one for showering; in fact, I detest getting wet. This is why I prefer riding in the desert Southwest. So I keep my diet clean so I don't smell like anything more than smoky coconut oil and salty wool, and only travel with one outfit. This is an extreme departure for most, I understand that, but it's still possible to apply this theory with a little bit of unlearning. What changed my life was wool underwear. Rivbike.com sells the MUSA variety with no seams on the taint area. They are great, and I'm unashamed to say that I wear the same pair every day until they wear out (about three to four months). I know a few others who do this also, so it's not totally crazy. You think our ancestors on horseback were doing laundry every night while Irish Springing their undercarriages? Now this method only works with a breathable leather saddle like the Brooks B17, for example. Also, get rid of all your synthetic clothing. Synthetic clothing can't be worn for more than a few hours without smelling like you augered face first into a vat of aged salad dressing. Synthetics are a bacterial orgy, and when it's not practical to wash yourself and your spandex every night, they should be avoided. Plus you won't have to pack any "casual clothes." My rule of thumb is if it doesn't stink, it's clean enough. I also "roast" my bare bottom over the hot coals of the campfire each night before tucking in. This ensures everything is good and dry down there.

Do you travel with a stove or stoveless?

Coming from backpacking, for the longest time I was most concerned about keeping my setups wicked light, so it was no stove with cold coconut milk and chia seeds every night. But as I've grown older and more epicurean, I've begun packing more cookable foods as well as a stove. Still, most of the time I cook on the fire. There is something very satisfying about cooking on the fire while staring into the dancing flames on a starry night. For me and my friends, fire is a crucial component of camping, and it's saddening that the very element that makes us human is criminalized in many places. It's for good reason, however, as most of us are so far removed from what fire even means. Learn how to respect and nurture a fire within a safe environment, and over time you'll be able to safely tend one wherever you may be, as long as it's outside California, obvs.

What is your preferred lightweight sleeping system?

I'm a big fan of the Mountain Laurel Designs Trailstar tarp. Look it up and you'll understand how versatile it is from the pictures and reviews. It can sleep three in a pinch and weighs no more than a bivy sack. I can pitch it in all sorts of different configurations, and also fit my bike underneath. Tarps are the best way to tell the world that you aren't an amateur. Plus they tend to blend into the environment, with their sacred geometry. That being said, if it's a short weeklong trip in the desert with no rain forecasted by the all-seeing gods of meteorology, I won't even bring a shelter. I always prefer to sleep out cowboy style at night. If it's in a non-desert environment where you get the morning dew, just make sure you're under a tree. All your stuff will stay dry that way. So my sleep system is a NeoAir XTherm (it's worth it), a Mountain Laurel Designs spirit quilt, and a ground cloth as a puncture barrier for my mattress. I also use an inflatable pillow with an Egyptian cotton pillowcase and a silk bag liner.

Anything else you'd like to add?

No matter what style or methodology your bike camping and touring setups reflect, we are all unified under the universal belief that immersing oneself on a bike in nature, whether it be 10 miles from home or the other side of Mars, is all the religion anyone needs. So go to church and light stuff on fire!

4.
BACKCOUNTRY SKILLS AND GEAR

Whether you're pushing miles, getting somewhere in the backcountry to relax, or just out wandering, basic gear and skills are necessary to thrive, and with an increased skill set typically comes a decreased reliance on gear. Refer to your established skills and comfort level when choosing gear for a trip—as your skills increase, you can strategically cut weight from your gear while remaining safe in case something unexpected occurs.

SKILLS VS. GEAR

Gear lists are great to help you prepare, organize, and visualize how much each item weighs and how you can remove or replace items to save weight. This type of list also helps to make sure you haven't forgotten anything and are fully prepared for the conditions that you may encounter. But don't just focus on your gear list when trying to cut weight. It is also essential to build your skills base.

Just like a gear list, think about creating a "Skills List" to help build and develop your skills before and during trips. This list should detail your abilities in both cycling and the outdoors. A skills list with an "if/then" column (if a tent pole snaps, then it can be fixed by applying a splint) can help determine gear choices. As you master additional skills, you'll be better prepared, gain confidence, and ultimately be able to pack less gear.

FIRST AID WITH MINIMAL SUPPLIES

Most first-aid kits contain a lot of extra "what-if" stuff. A first-aid kit can vary by location, nature, and duration of the trip. There are a few items that always remain the same, but quantities will change depending on distance, and other items will get inserted or deleted due to various factors. Keep in mind that if anything major happens, your first-aid skills will likely only be a small step in the process of maintaining comfort, keeping life functions stable, and doing no further harm while seeking a higher level of care as quickly as possible.

Here are some details on how to minimize your kit while still being prepared for most situations.

Training

Whether it's just basic first aid or a full Wilderness First Responder (WFR) course, training will help you become comfortable tending to injuries while traveling by bike. With the purpose and goal in mind, you can create the solution with the supplies you have with you and in your surroundings. In the backcountry, there's only so much you can do to help an injury no matter how much equipment you have. You learn to make do with what you have, with the ultimate first-aid goals being: 1) do no further harm, 2) patient comfort, and 3) transport quickly and efficiently to a higher level of care.

Proactive Versus Reactive

One important factor that helps to pare down a first-aid kit is being proactive to any issues that might arise instead of reactive. Plan trips knowing, among other details, how long between resupplies, potential exit points, typical conditions, and temperatures. This helps to prepare you for any potential emergencies that you might face. For example, you are not likely to have frostbite or acute mountain sickness during the summer while in the canyon country in Utah, but you can encounter heat exhaustion and dehydration. Knowing this ahead of your trip will allow you to pack the appropriate items: sunscreen, oral rehydration solution, plenty of water, etc.

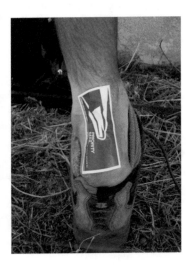

Ultralight is using whatever you can find and geting creative with what you have. In this case I grabbed a couple of stickers from the post office to prevent any additional damage and take precautions against blisters. JUSTIN LICHTER

Being alone in the backcountry requires the ability to care for yourself, no matter what unexpected scenario might occur.

By stopping at the first instances of pain to assess the situation, you can often prevent an injury from getting worse or becoming completely debilitating. Adjusting your seat height for knee pain, applying chamois cream for skin irritation, or taping a spot rubbing on your foot before a full-blown blister develops can go a long way.

Location and Duration

Location plays a large role in determining the contents of a first-aid kit. Will you be touring in the United States? Will you be in Africa, Nepal, or South America? What are you going to find in those countries and what risks are present? Will you be able to restock items if needed once you are in that country? In parts of Africa and Southeast Asia, malaria medicine is crucial. In other places, preventive medicine for waterborne illnesses may be necessary. How much time will it take to get to the closest resupply town with a supermarket, pharmacy, or doctor?

The duration of the trip and the duration between resupply are also important to determine how much of each item you need to transport before reaching the safety of society and a place where you can restock meds or supplies. Carry enough of what you think you need to get you to the next opportunity to restock.

A Simple First-Aid Kit

Item	Use
Ibuprofen	To relieve pain and swelling
Bandanna or clothes	To make slings, compression wraps, and act as a buffer for icing injuries/swelling
Sandwich bag	To ice injuries (with snow, ice, or cold water). Can be used as an occlusive dressing, and for food storage.
Needle and thread	To make slings, repairs, or alterations in the field
Small knife/multi-tool	To cut fabric and other items, and tend to blisters
Bike	To lean on like crutches to help take weight off an injured leg while walking
Seatpost or tree branch	To splint a broken bone or damaged joint
Bandages	To cover exposed wounds
Duct tape	To care for foot or finger issues, and repair gear

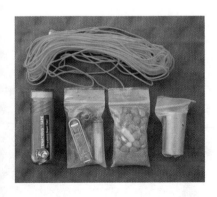

Simple first-aid and gear repair kit (ibuprofen, a few glucosamine pills, duct tape, cord, Tenacious Tape, multi-tool, needle and thread). JUSTIN LICHTER

Other Considerations

For traveling internationally to developing countries, it's best to fill prescriptions before leaving and consider bringing medications for diarrhea, upset stomach, wound infections, and bacterial infections (e.g., Imodium, Pepto-Bismol tablets, Cipro, Azithromycin, Tinidazole, triple antibiotic ointment, etc.). Rip duct tape, and similar items, from the main roll to create a smaller roll, and repackage medications into small baggies to save weight and space.

CAMPSITE SELECTION

Camping under the stars can make for a perfect ending to a long day in the saddle, particularly when you have the option of choosing your ideal campsite. In some cases local laws, private property, or finding stealth roadside coverage may dictate where you lie to rest for the night, but more often than not there are numerous options for where to lay a ground cloth and doze off. Choosing a

good campsite is critical, as it allows you to trim down from a "bombproof" tent to an ultralight tarp or lighter-weight tent while remaining fully functional. A good campsite also lets you choose a sleeping bag and sleep system that will be lighter and sufficient for the conditions. Here's what you should look for in a good camping spot:

- Follow Leave No Trace ethics by avoiding meadows, fragile vegetation, and setting up in close proximity to water sources.

- Consider a location that keeps your bike out of sight and enables you to secure it to your shelter or a tree.

- In well-traveled areas, many impacted campsites are along riverbanks, shorelines, lakes, saddles, and other flat areas. These are often great places to camp since you won't be impacting a new site. Previously used sites are often chosen for their proximity to water sources and trees, meaning you can carry less water weight and have reliable structure for anchoring a tarp shelter.

- Keep in mind that air settles around lakes and low points, which can make it colder than camping in a forest. Large water sources also produce moist air and an increased concentration of bugs, both of which can cause undesirable effects if your lightweight shelter does not protect from condensation or biting insects.

- Insects are best avoided in dry open areas with a breeze, such as on a ridgeline or saddle. You can also—if it's safe—start a small smoke fire to ward them off.

- When you know you're sleeping in or setting up a multiday base camp, try to set up in a shady spot. It keeps your tent cooler and, by avoiding UV radiation, helps the fabrics last longer.

- In windy conditions face the narrow part of your tent or shelter into the wind. It reduces wind noise and the chances that the shelter will be broadsided, which can keep you up all night.

- Avoid depressions or low spots, and consider places where water might run off and pool under your shelter if it rained overnight. This is even more important when sleeping in a canyon—make sure you're not pitched in a spot that could get hit by a flash flood. If you think it may rain or flash flood, make sure you have an exit route in mind.

- When camping on a previously undisturbed spot, try to minimize your impact by putting things like rocks, branches, pine needles, etc., back where you found them in the morning. Try to make it look like no one has camped there, which minimizes the chance that someone else will see it and use the spot as a campsite. We want to make sure it won't become another impacted campsite—there are enough of them already.

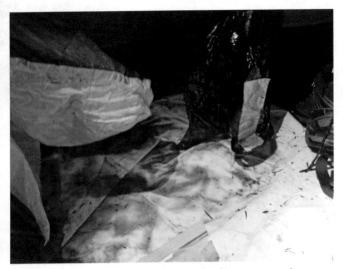

Regretting our campsite decision. After a night of heavy rain, waking up in a puddle of water when camping in a bad spot is a rude awakening.
JUSTIN LICHTER

- Ultralight ground cloths, shelters, and sleeping pads are delicate, so be sure to "sweep" away any sharp objects, including pinecones, rocks, pine needles, etc., before setting up.

- The simplest and often most enjoyable setup is sleeping under the stars. It's also easy to take down. Your unused shelter makes a great pillow and leaves an unobstructed view of the night sky.

By planning and selecting an ideal campsite, you can often minimize cold and wet conditions and sleep warmer. In doing so, you will also sleep better and be

more comfortable. Plus, you'll be able to shed some ounces by carrying a lighter sleeping bag, shelter, and layering system. Knowing how to choose a good campsite and setting up and using your shelter confidently can give way to lighter shelters and ultralight tarps. Ultimately you learn what shelter is preferred for specific trips and seasons, and invariably become efficient with setup and takedown even in adverse conditions.

NAVIGATION

Knowing how to use a map and compass are critical skills. When seeking out the road, trail, or path less (or not yet) traveled, navigation becomes an important skill crucial to keeping your adventure on track. Navigating with a map requires staying on top of your current location and knowing about obvious upcoming features. Peaks, rivers, cliffs, and other distinct features will show up on the map and

help you pinpoint your location should you get in a pre-
dicament. Navigating with a map and compass is a skill
you should know before you head out in the backcountry.
When traveling ultralight without navigational tools, keep
the following skills in mind:

To determine the amount of daylight remaining as the
sun approaches the horizon at the end of the day, cover the
sun with your thumb, palm facing you. Each finger above
the horizon represents 10 to 15 minutes before sunset.

If you aren't carrying a compass, you can use the sun
to determine direction using the hour hands of an analog
watch face or by placing a stick in the ground.

- In the Northern Hemisphere the sun is due south
  at noon (it's easier to tell before and after summer,
  when the sun travels lower in the sky). In the Southern
  Hemisphere the sun is due north at noon; again it's
  easier to tell when the sun's lower in the sky. When
  using an analog watch in the Northern Hemisphere
  to determine direction, point the hour hand in the
  direction of the sun, keeping the watch face flat.
  Halfway between the hour hand and the 12 is south.
  So if it's 5 p.m. in the Northern Hemisphere, south
  would be between 8 and 9. North is opposite of
  that. In the Southern Hemisphere, point the 12 on the
  watch face toward the sun. Halfway between the 12
  and the hour hand is north.

- Alternatively, you can place a stick about 3 feet tall
  or something else upright in the ground. Mark the
  location at the end of the shadow. Wait about 20

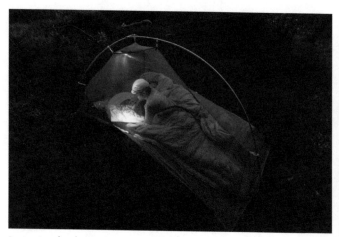
Reviewing the day's progress and plotting your course for the next day can be a relaxing way to wind down an evening in the backcountry.

minutes and mark the tip of the shadow again. Draw a line connecting the two marks. This shows you an approximate east to west direction; you can calculate north and south by drawing a perpendicular line.

This may seem trivial, but paper weight adds up—make sure to cut off white space around maps to save weight and fit properly into waterproof pouches, print double sided when possible, or use detailed photographs of a map on an electronic device that you may already be carrying, such as a smartphone.

When piecing together off-road routes, it may be difficult to determine distances between trail junctions or calculate other unknown distances. To do so, hold a string to the map's scale and mark it to match miles, half miles, and

other intervals as needed. You can then use the string to measure distances on the map, which will give you a fairly accurate measure of the trail's distance.

GOING LIGHT WITH YOUR OFF-THE-BIKE GEAR

With the essential elements of trip planning in place and your skills bolstered, a proper kit for the proposed terrain, remoteness, weather conditions, and duration can be assembled. Remember, "proper prior planning prevents piss poor performance." This goes a long way in figuring out what equipment will be invaluable for certain trips and what will be extraneous. Think of your kit as a Mr. Potato Head: Each piece of gear is interchangeable and can be adapted or chosen based on the type of trip and the conditions you will likely encounter.

Sleep System

A lightweight sleep system entails your sleeping pad and sleeping bag or quilt, with optional items such as a liner or pillow (best made from your clothing and a stuff sack). One of the easiest ways to save weight and bulk is by packing a sleeping bag with an appropriate temperature rating for the intended conditions. Overly warm bags add not only ounces but also a notable increase in volume that can be troublesome to fit within the confines of frame bags, sometimes requiring additional carrying capacity, which further compounds weight gain.

Sleeping bag: For all bikepacking and bike touring trips, a high-quality down sleeping bag or quilt is best suited. Down is much lighter and more packable than synthetics. You can pack your sleeping bag either in a waterproof stuff sack or trash bag so it is fully protected throughout the day and not vulnerable to water.

Whenever possible unpack your sleeping bag when you first stop for the night instead of waiting until getting ready to sleep. This allows the bag more time to decompress so it can re-loft. If it's nice out during the day, air out your sleeping bag during a break. This will help keep it dry and lofty for when you need it later when it's potentially cold, wet, and won't dry out.

If you need to purchase your first sleeping bag or only have one bag in your quiver, consider what time of year and where you will most likely be touring. For most people a 20-degree bag is a good temperature rating that will work for most of the year. If you sleep warm and wear clothing layers while sleeping, then a 30-degree bag can

The Accomplice down quilt from Enlightened Equipment is available in a variety of configurations and is an excellent choice when bikepacking with your partner.

be sufficient as a three-season bag. For summer-only pursuits consider a bag with a rating of 45 degrees or above, or just a lightweight liner. A lightweight silk liner is also perfect when the trip entails traveling from hotel to hotel, hut to hut, or hostel to hostel. The liner can act as a barrier between you and grimy surfaces in these situations and packs down really small.

An ultralight down quilt, such as those from Enlightened Equipment and Katabatic Gear, save weight by cutting out the portion of the sleeping bag underneath your body where the loft is compressed and theoretically not adding any warmth. Many of these quilts have a cinch or strap system to help keep it in place on the sleeping pad. Otherwise there is a propensity for the quilt to shift and let in drafts since it does not continuously wrap underneath you. When utilizing a quilt, it can be handy to add an ultralight bivy to the system to help keep the burrito'd components in place, prevent drafts, and add about 5 to 10 degrees of warmth. If you move around a lot in your sleep, keep in mind that a quilt is more susceptible to allowing cold air to enter.

Your shelter will dictate how exposed to the elements you are and play a large part in the warmth of your sleep system. A fully enclosed tent will typically add around 10 degrees to your sleep system since it keeps warmer air inside and also provides a barrier against any wind, but will add a pound or several to your load depending upon the size.

Using a quilt on a chilly night. JUSTIN LICHTER

Sleeping pad: There are multiple varieties of sleeping pads. The single most important factor in choosing a sleeping pad is picking one that you are going to sleep well on. It's not worth saving a few ounces if you are unable to sleep. Being well rested improves your recovery and your enjoyment.

With current sleeping pad technology you can get a very comfortable pad, with a relatively high R-value (insulation factor) that packs down to the size of a 1-liter Nalgene. An inflatable pad is advisable since they are more packable and lighter than standard foam pads. Plus they offer an increased R-value, comfort, and thickness to cushion your hips and shoulders from the ground if you are a side sleeper. Current inflatable pads, like the Thermarest Neo-Air, provide a comfort-to-weight ratio that is hard to beat.

A nice sleeping pad can allow you to sleep almost anywhere, even on the floor of the Bishkek airport.

If you choose to use a sleeping pad that is less than full length to save weight, you can remove your bar bag or seat bag—or use your backpack—and put it underneath your legs to serve as the lower portion of your sleep system and help insulate you from the ground.

With an inflatable pad that has a thickness of over an inch, some people find it more comfortable to blow up the pad the entire amount and then let a little bit of air out. This will allow the pad to conform to your body when you lie on it.

Pillow: Use the stuff sack or trash bag that you packed your sleeping bag in as your pillowcase, filling it with any spare clothes you have to make it your preferred height. This eliminates the need to carry a pillow and keeps your clothes a bit warmer for chilly early morning starts.

If a low temperature is pushing the limits of your sleeping bag rating, plan to wear your extra clothes to sleep, including a beanie, gloves, and socks. The first area of your body likely to get cold is your feet, which can be remedied by sleeping with your down jacket (or other insulating layers) in the footbox of your sleeping bag with your feet in the sleeves. You can also boil water and place it in a well-sealed water bottle in the lower part of your sleeping bag to add warmth.

Make sure you use your sleeping bag as it was intended by cinching the mummy hood and draft collar to keep the warm air in and prevent drafts. Avoid breathing inside the sleeping bag since this creates moisture inside your bag and may decrease some loft in the down.

Consuming a warm meal before a long, cold night at elevation.

A few other tips for a little extra warmth on a cold night:

- Find a campsite out of the wind and away from water.

- Urinate before going to sleep. This helps to keep your body warm.

- Eat a snack before sleeping.

- Sleep on your side.

- Pull your beanie down as far as it will go on your head.

Full-length sleeping pad sleep system with extra clothes filling a stuff sack for the pillow. JUSTIN LICHTER

Using a half-length sleeping pad with your backpack as the lower half.
JUSTIN LICHTER

After pedaling all day, it's good to elevate your legs at night. This can also help with recovery as it drains fluid buildup in your legs and feet. Consider using your food bag (when not in bear country) or other ancillary items, putting them on the lower portion of your sleeping pad.

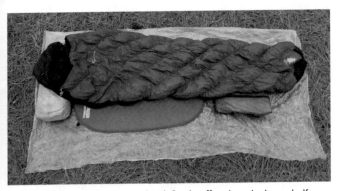

Using a half-length sleeping pad with food stuff sack as the lower half.
JUSTIN LICHTER

This will usually create just enough lift to be comfortable but also sufficient rise for recovery.

Shelter

Shelters come in a variety of forms, from full-scale four-season tents to ultra-lightweight Cuben Fiber (non-woven Dyneema) tarps. There are a range of features and designs available. For bikepacking, a flat tarp that can be set up in a variety of ways, including an A-frame or lean-to, is ideal. This style packs the smallest and is easiest to set up between two trees or using your bike as an anchor. It also provides the most space for the weight. For additional protection there are bug inserts made specifically to fit under this shape of tarp. On the other hand, pyramid-shaped tarps are better at dealing with wind and stormy weather, but you'll need some sort of pole to support the middle of the shelter. For that reason, A-frame tarps are most convenient.

Other potential lightweight shelters are tarptents, single-walled tents, and compact double-walled tents.

A tarptent is similar to a traditional tent but is single-walled or a hybrid style, meaning the rain protection layer is the main layer in places. There usually isn't an overlap of nylon and mesh throughout the whole body of the tent. This often shaves a lot of weight, but can also lead to increased condensation depending on the climate and the conditions. Some tarptents can be set up without a tent pole, saving even more weight, but make sure to research the design carefully to see if this is a possibility. You'll likely have to use your bike and/or trees or other objects to tie off to for setup.

A single-walled shelter can be useful in a dry climate that is less likely to have condensation. In wet or humid environments, they are prone to condensation buildup. The single wall saves weight by not duplicating fabric, but is noticeably less breathable and often requires a tent pole for support.

A double-walled shelter is a full tent, typically with a netting interior and a rainfly. There are some very light options for double-walled tents now, like the Big Agnes Fly Creek Platinum. These can be useful in mosquito or buggy areas, and are definitely recommended for international trips in developing countries as they will provide a bit more cover, privacy, and security. They will also give you more flexibility—a freestanding or nearly freestanding shelter that you can set up just about anywhere flat.

The downfall of many tarptents and traditional tents is that a pole is needed for setup. You can fasten these fairly

easily to your handlebar bag to keep them relatively out of the way, but it is still an extra piece of equipment to deal with on a daily basis that ultimately adds weight.

Tarps are the lightest and most packable shelter option. Not those sold at Wal-Mart and hardware stores, but rather specialized outdoor shelters that come in a variety of fabrics, shapes, and sizes. The typical and most affordable ultralight fabric is silnylon (silicone-impregnated nylon). This is fairly durable for its weight and is waterproof, although it's best to seal the seam(s) before use. Lighter than silnylon is Spinnaker and Cuben Fiber. Spinnaker tends to lose its water repellency faster than silnylon and Cuben Fiber. Cuben Fiber is very lightweight and also very durable for its weight, but much more expensive.

A tarp saves the additional weight of a fabric floor and instead allows you to incorporate a lightweight polycro

Flat tarp set up A-frame style between two trees. This type of setup gives good coverage so we are ready for the impending thunderstorm.
JUSTIN LICHTER

Using the bike to help set up a silnylon flat tarp as an A-frame. JUSTIN LICHTER

Taking a break from riding and from the relentless mosquitoes in an ultralight tent in the Canadian Rockies. Choose your shelter based on the weather conditions you will likely encounter, and don't forget to take into account if it's bug season. JUSTIN LICHTER

groundsheet or piece of Tyvek, which only weights 1 to 3 ounces, to go under your sleep system to protect your pad and keep your gear dry.

Cooking Kit

The lightest cooking kit is the one left behind. Committing to a stoveless setup can save considerable volume and weight in your kit, but is best saved for trips where food is abundant, appetizing, and inexpensive. Cooking a warm meal at the end of the day is rewarding and provides variety to your diet, which can be easily taken for granted, so be sure to test out going cook-less on a short trip before committing to it for a longer journey.

When campfires are permitted, a condensed stoveless cooking kit can be assembled with minimal components, but for most journeys a self-sufficient cooking kit entails a stove, fuel, pot, lighter (or matches), and eating utensil. In summer months a 0.9-liter pot is generally sufficient for one person, depending on the size of your appetite and what you plan on cooking. In the winter a 1.3-liter pot is better

Thai street food at its finest.

Reflecting on the day's adventures and wondering what tomorrow will bring while enjoying dinner prepared on the campfire.

suited since the added volume allows for bigger meals/ more calories and has more area to melt snow. When shaving weight from your cooking kit, there is nothing that can compare to a titanium pot. It is the lightest and strongest material on the market. Granted it is not the best at heat transfer and it is expensive, but it is by far the best option if you are counting grams. Grab a titanium spork, or a ti spoon, to use as your eating utensil, an alcohol stove, and a mini BiC lighter to round out the ultimate lightweight cooking kit.

For cooking consider an alcohol stove as a simple, lightweight, quiet, and compact solution. There is nothing to go wrong, break, or clean. Simply pour alcohol in the stove and light it. It burns slowly and will boil water in a reasonable amount of time, but those requiring morning coffee or who enjoy boiling water more than once per day may want to use a canister stove for its ease of use; otherwise an alcohol stove should suffice for most cooking needs. You can also make your own alcohol stove out of soda cans, tuna cans, or cat food cans. You can't beat that price!

Some alcohol stoves, like the Trail Designs Ti Tri, are packable and extremely efficient, even in windy conditions. Keep in mind that in some locations, such as in Southern California, alcohol stoves may be included in fire restrictions during the summer months. Check local regulations during trip planning if you have any concerns.

In the United States, look for Heet, the gas-line antifreeze in the yellow bottle. It's methyl alcohol, which burns

Using a Trail Designs Ti Tri alcohol stove in the winter, despite many people believing that alcohol stoves don't work well in the cold. JUSTIN LICHTER

Fueling up before heading into a remote stretch of the Tien Shen Mountains.

cleanly and is cheaper than denatured alcohol. You can also use denatured alcohol and rubbing alcohol if you're desperate, but it blows out easily and blackens your pot.

Finding denatured alcohol internationally is not as difficult as many people think, and we've found access to it in dozens of countries to date. Keep in mind you really just want methyl alcohol, which in many countries is used as a window cleaning fluid, just dyed purple so people won't drink it.

Consider keeping your alcohol fuel in a flexible 0.5-liter soft water bottle. This isn't necessary but works better than a hard-sided water bottle. As you deplete your fuel, it will shrink in size and become more packable within frame bags.

While multi-fuel stoves are not recommended for the majority of trips since they are heavier and can be temperamental, they can be invaluable in developing countries where traditional camping stove fuels, denatured/methyl alcohol, or canisters are hard to come by. The beauty of the multi-fuel stove is that you can use unleaded gasoline, kerosene, or white gas, so you are more likely to find some type of fuel to use when you are running low. If you plan to use anything other than white gas, make sure you know how to properly clean your stove and reassemble it. The stove will get gunked up fairly often when you use alternate fuels. Your pot will also get blackened from the soot.

As you get proficient with using your multi-fuel stove, consider lightening it up by removing the legs and using your titanium tent pegs to stabilize the pot above the flame—just make sure the stove body is balanced when cooking. This may not seem like it would reduce the weight substantially, but on some models this change alone can reduce the weight by a third!

Also, if you are traveling in a group and think you'll need multiple fuel bottles, it can be lighter and more packable to use the smallest hard-sided fuel bottle and pump available and refill that bottle as needed rather than trying to pack a larger volume.

When cooking, keep the lid on your pot while heating your food or boiling water to minimize cooking times. This also uses less fuel and water, so you won't need to carry as much water throughout the day. You can also minimize water and fuel requirements, and cut down on cooking times, by soaking certain foods beforehand.

Cooking the night away in Kyrgyzstan. *Bon appétit!*

When choosing cooking gear, keep in mind packability since frame bags limit volume and can make fitting large, rigid items awkward. If it works with your packing system, choose a pot that's wider than it is taller. This allows more contact area with the flame, increasing efficiency, and helps lower the cook system's center of gravity, which increases stability.

Water and Water Treatment

At 2.2 pounds per liter, water is one of the heaviest items you need to carry, so having the ability to locate or create safe drinking water on the go is invaluable. Despite the appearance of a pristine backcountry stream, there are countless unseen variables that may cause a source to be contaminated, ultimately resulting in a waterborne illness. Most water treatment options weigh just 6 ounces or

Refilling our water supply while overlooking Afghanistan.
JUSTIN KLINE

considerably less, so they can add protection and save the weight of carrying additional water, with minimal added weight to your kit.

Key factors for evaluating water treatment methods are effectiveness, speed, weight, size, pore size (only relevant for filters), convenience and ease of use, maintenance, lifespan and durability, impact on taste, and cost. Keep in mind that some filters do not have a small enough pore size to capture viruses. This is not a problem in the United States, since the water sources do not have viruses, but can be internationally. Here are three common lightweight treatment solutions with proven success.

Chemical treatment: Aqua Mira, a chlorine dioxide system, is the most common ultralight chemical treatment. It has two dropper bottles, and you mix the droppers per the instructions in the cap. When it turns yellow you dump it in your water bottle. Average weight is only 1 to 2 ounces. You can treat various amounts of water—for instance, if you are carrying a hydration bladder—by tailoring the treatment. Aqua Mira does slightly change the taste of the water and takes about 30 minutes until the water is considered treated. This lightweight system packs up very small, and you can adjust how much you take with you by repackaging in smaller dropper bottles if you are out on shorter trips. Chemical treatments can also work as hand sanitizer in a pinch. It is worth noting that chemicals take longer to treat cold water than warm water. In addition, it takes longer to treat viruses and cysts with chemicals because they have "thick shells." If you're at a nasty-looking water source, you might want to treat it twice or let the chemicals sit longer than the recommendation.

UV treatment: A SteriPEN uses ultraviolet light to treat water, which is a safe and proven technology used by many municipal water departments. The various "pen" models weigh just 2.6 to 6 ounces depending on the battery source. The beauty of the SteriPEN is that the water is treated nearly instantaneously. It only takes 45 seconds for a half liter and 90 seconds for a liter. There won't be any change of taste or temperature, and the SteriPEN has a safety mechanism that automatically shuts the UV light off when it is removed from the water.

The micro USB-rechargeable SteriPEN Ultra is lightweight, simple to use, and works well when using bike bottles.

The SteriPEN weighs slightly more, but when you consider the flexibility and instant gratification, it clearly makes up for the added weight. The low-volume size and shape is also compatible with frame bag carrying systems, and it's easily tucked away in a side pocket for convenient access throughout the day.

Inline treatment: The Sawyer filter is a small inline filter that treats water as it's drawn from a water bottle or hydration bladder. Sawyer has a couple of models that weigh between an ounce and 4 ounces. They are very lightweight and packable, and provide a simple system for water treatment and instant gratification. Your water will be ready as soon as it passes through the filter, no matter if it is cold or warm. Most importantly, there will be no change of taste or chemicals needed.

Other Water Considerations

Carry the appropriate amount of water by knowing how far away the next certain water source is. Drink up at each water source to rehydrate. If it is a long stretch between sources, you may want to "camel up" at the water source before setting out. When you're super hydrated, you likely won't need to drink much of your water for at least an hour or more, thereby allowing you to carry less water for the stretch and save weight.

Depending on the location of the trip, you'll likely want the ability to carry a minimum of 2 liters (assuming you can access water regularly en route). Carrying any less is typically just a nuisance since you'll be forced to refill within a short time frame. For long-distance water carrying requirements, consider soft-sided carrying options offered by Platypus and MSR, since they can take the shape of where they are packed, and are compact and virtually weightless when empty.

Keep in mind that many illnesses contracted in the backcountry are blamed on contaminated water when in fact they're often caused by poor hygiene, improper hand washing, or cross-contamination from others, so it's equally as important to maintain basic hygiene.

Clothing Kit

The key to a perfect bikepacking clothing kit is comfort and versatility, not only while riding but also when off the bike. When dealing with a limited wardrobe, it's essential to layer clothes effectively. Ideally your clothing system is an integrated component of your entire kit, meaning layers are utilized not only during the day but also as part of establishing a warm overnight kit. If a clothing garment can be used in only a specific climate or situation and has not been used within a couple of days on a trip, then it is likely not worth carrying next time around.

Clothing is typically the most overpacked item on trips, so it's important to establish a solid layering system that allows you to carry less while being prepared for a variety of weather conditions, and gives you the ability to adjust on the go. When left with the choice, consider ditching a full change of clothes in favor of additional layers. This adds versatility to your layering system and decreases weight. With just a single base layer, insulating layer, and outer layer, you can travel comfortably in a variety of climates.

Base layer: Essentially the piece of clothing that is almost always on your skin. A functional base layer should be comfortable, breathable, and move moisture (sweat) from your body, ideally while remaining relatively odor

To each his own. Soaking in the sun while wearing a variety of layers.

free. The amount of base layer coverage is personal preference and will likely be dictated by your touring destination
and season, but typically an ideal base layer is a lightweight merino wool T-shirt. Consider a half-zip long-sleeve
to protect from the sun, provide additional warmth, man-
age moisture, and regulate temperature with minimal odor.

Arm and knee (or leg) warmers provide ideal versatility to a three-season clothing kit. They are lightweight,
easily packable, and can be thrown on or taken off quickly
and on the go to help regulate body temperature.

Bottom layer: For most bikepackers and lightweight
touring cyclists, consecutive full days in the saddle require
the use of a chamois. If that's the case, choose your favorite and roll with it, but resist the temptation to bring more
than one spare chamois. They can be cleaned daily with
soap and water or even baby wipes, so traveling with one

or two pairs can be comfortable and add minimal weight to your clothing kit. Going chamois-less is another option for minimizing the clothing burden, and is particularly

Fabric Selection

After years of use with a full gamut of fiber choices, merino wool comes out as the clear choice for a daily-worn base layer, and for other layers when available. Its combination of comfort and performance for moisture management and odor elimination are unmatched. Traveling with limited garments will inevitably result in a less than appealing smell. Forget synthetic wicking garments, cotton, technical base layers, and everything else with claims to performance. For everyday garments on and off the bike, merino wool offers superior properties for odor resistance, wicking performance, and drying speed with above-average durability.

Utilizing a leather saddle, like those from Brooks, can open up the opportunity for going chamois-less, even over the long haul.

feasible when you are riding a leather saddle, such as the Brooks B17, which adapts to the shape of your body over time. When doing so, consider wicking and wool underwear such as those from ExOfficio and rivbike.com for improved comfort, temperature regulation, and odor resistance over time. In either case a relatively lightweight and quick-drying over short is useful off the bike, for sleeping and as a bathing suit.

Insulating layer/mid-layer: The insulating layer, or mid-layer, is a versatile layer that's key to the layering system and will vary depending upon the season and nature of the trip. Consider a single long-sleeved wool garment or a down- or synthetic-filled jacket, based upon the conditions you will be facing. The packability and weight of a high-loft ultralight down micro-puff is hard to beat, but

Enjoying the view of the Pamir Mountains, and the warmth and versatility of a wool sweater. A garment doesn't have to be marketed as technical to perform well; it just has to be made from the right material.

wool- or synthetic-based insulation will do a better job of maintaining warmth when wet.

Wind layer: A lightweight wind jacket or vest can be a useful layer while riding and be extremely packable and weigh as little as 39 grams. The lightweight wind barrier can add a surprising amount of warmth on chilly descents, during cool and inclement weather, and when your body is cooling down during a break, by holding core body heat in and blocking cool air out. A lightweight wind-blocking vest or jacket should be form fitting to avoid flapping in the wind while riding.

Outer layer: For most trips a protective outer shell is crucial since it safeguards from wind, rain, and snow. It should keep your inner layers from getting wet and allow you to retain a comfortable level of body heat through protection

Traveling light with a single outer shell for wind and rain protection, and long descents.

and ventilation. A shell layer that doesn't breathe adequately and ventilate can leave you just as wet from sweat as you would be from precipitation. A hard shell provides far more protection from the elements then a lightweight wind layer, so when looking to condense your clothing kit, consider utilizing your waterproof/breathable rain shell for weather protection, wind protection, and warmth, rather than carrying a separate windproof layer and rain shell.

Look for a shell jacket equipped with a hood, and make sure it will fit over your bike helmet. A covered head will provide significantly more comfort when you are dealing with 8 hours of riding in the rain, and will help prevent your base layers from becoming saturated.

Footwear: Clipless pedals or platform pedals? That is always the question. Once your personal preference is established, it's simply a matter of committing to a comfortable clip-in or casual sneaker. The biggest consideration is finding a shoe that is not only comfortable in the pedals but also off the bike when pushing, resupplying, and camping. The bulk and weight of a second set of shoes is best left behind when possible, but a lightweight pair of flip-flops or compact pair of down booties, depending upon the season, can make for happy feet when spending time at camp.

Getting creative to create extra warmth. If your toes are getting extremely cold, use what you have with you. In this case I'm using a gallon-size ziplock bag to create an ultralight, low-budget, vapor-barrier liner to keep body heat in.
JUSTIN LICHTER

An ideal layering system evolves over time, but with only the items above, you can create a versatile system that can provide comfort in almost any three-season weather scenario. Even in continually cold and wet conditions where warm shelter and heat is inaccessible for days, you can maintain the same layering system, since the merino wool or synthetic mid-layer will continue to insulate even when wet. At the end of the day, you can sleep with the base layers on or in your sleeping bag to help dry them out. In the morning wet rain gear layers can be put back on since your body is insulated from them and will soon be generating heat once riding. If you've been soaked all day, make sure to strip off the wet layers as soon as you stop for the day and have set up your shelter. Then immediately change into any remaining layers or get into your

Winter and high alpine pursuits often require adding down layers to your clothing kit.

sleeping bag to warm up, before attempting to dry layers for the night using your body heat.

Food

Nutrition is one of the most important considerations when you are riding for hours and days on end. Proper nourishment, budgeting, and packaging will provide sustenance and save weight, allowing you to travel more efficiently and carry less, all while providing the calories and nutrition required to energize your trip and fuel recovery.

No matter what your taste buds desire—salty chips, cured meats, peanut butter, burritos, or energy bars—all food can be measured and boiled down to calories per ounce when determining how much of it your body requires. When riding for an extended period of time, your metabolic rate will substantially increase, so it's important to seek nutrient-rich, calorie-dense, good-tasting food that you won't get tired of.

A well-fed bikepacker is a happy bikepacker.

The more calories per ounce, the less food weight you may have to carry. Many foods weigh in at 150 calories per ounce or higher. For instance, on the high end of the spectrum, olive oil and ghee are close to 250 calories per ounce. Carbohydrates and protein have about 100 calories per ounce, while fat has up to 250 calories per ounce. Food that's less than 110 calories per ounce isn't ideal because you must carry extra food weight, and anything under 110 calories per ounce is likely composed of water weight, which is heavy and has no calories.

If incorporating math equations into your diet is your thing, shoot for foods with greater than 120 calories per ounce. When attempting to meet a 4,000-calorie-per-day diet, you'd only have to carry 2 pounds of food per day. When riding day after day sunup to sundown on a strenuous trip, it's easy to burn well over 4,000 calories in a day, but consuming that amount of calories can be sufficient to sustain energy over the short-term. For extended trips you'll likely have to start increasing your food weight to 2.5 to 3 pounds per day. Don't let numbers cloud your judgment when it comes to food weight though. Carrying insufficient rations or not eating frequently enough will cause you to lose weight, energy, and motivation. Additional food weight will decrease substantially each day as it's consumed, and on all but the most remote rides can be resupplied at least weekly, if not sooner.

When shopping for food during resupply or before you start a trip, be organized and think in terms of meals to help determine quantity. Remember, weight, size, and packaging of the food you choose is important when fitting it into bikepacking bags. Also consider the ease of preparation when choosing food, since you'll likely be tired at night and want a quick, easy meal.

You can't always get what you want, but sometimes you just might find you get what you need.

Taste is crucial. You don't want to eat food you don't like after a long day of riding. Bland off-the-shelf freeze-dried meals can be replaced by cobbling things together from bulk items and other normal food choices in a grocery store. There are plenty of other easy-to-prepare—and cheaper—meals available in the supermarket. For example, foods like tuna come in plastic packets, which are handy for camping. Cans are heavy, less convenient for packing out, and usually contain added liquid that adds a lot of extra water weight, not calories, to your food.

Breakfast of champions in Central Asia.

Fresh yogurt found trailside in the Swiss Alps is tough to beat.

Foraging at Its Finest by @ultraromance

There is no denying that the lightest, and some of the tastiest, meals are those made from fresh ingredients found along the way. Here @ultraromance provides some insight on assembling a scrumptious supper from foraged ingredients and a few key fixings worth keeping in your bikepacking pantry.

Poppi's Power Pauper Trail Goulash

Bouillon cubes are cheap, tasty, packable, and versatile . . . kinda . . . I always have 'em adorning my camp kitchen, and have them incidentally seasoning the bottoms of my stuff sacks. I'm always like "are those my spare socks I'm smelling?? Aww, yah, that's a bouillon cube onion waft." It's exciting.

Coconut oil: The praises of coconut oil have been heard by all, and for the most part are all true. It's incredibly stable at high temperatures while cooking, and won't go bad in yer camp kitchen.

Other uses:

- It's antibacterial and antimicrobial. A great alternative to showering.

- Brush yer teeth with it. Seriously!

- Service yer undercarriage and keep saddle sores at bay.

- Moisturize yer Brooks saddle.

- Keep a beach olfactory atmosphere going through the wintär.

For yer protein, I recommend tempeh for the vegetarians, and high-quality venison or bison jerky for carnivores.

Micronutrients needn't be packed in. They're everywhere you look, and far more nutritious than anything you can buy at the store. Weeds brü.

Choice:

- Lamb's-quarter (like spinach, but better)

- Nettle

- Watercress

- Sheep sorrel

Not so choice, but good for you:

- Dandelion (It's everywhere, and makes kale's nutrition label read like iceberg lettuce. Plus, since when did you eat kale for the taste anyway?)

- Common plantain (not bananas)

- Basically anything green. It's nearly impossible to poison yourself with greens. Trust your instincts. Try a corner of something, and if it makes your mouth do somersaults, you probably shouldn't eat it. It's how we've managed for 12,000 years until about 150 years ago. You may be a computer nerd with spindly fingers and translucent visage, but you still have the DNA of a *great warrior*.

Finally your carbo. For a quick and easy one, add one or two prebaked sweet potatoes. Just chop 'em up. Two quick-cooking (10 to 15 minutes) options are quinoa and millet.

OK, here's what to do:

- Get your ti bowl on the stove or fire.
- Add a cup of water.
- Add a bouillon cube.
- Simmer down from a boil.
- Add an ancient antique grain (optional), add coconut oil, and cover.
- Simmer for 10 minutes and add protein and chopped greens.
- Cook for another 5 to 7.23 minutes and add the baked sweet potatoes.

FIN!

The best resource is to just eat little nibbles of things you see a lot of along the way. If it tastes weird, don't eat it. Through evolution, our senses are incredibly perceptive, but underutilized in the grocery store world. I'm not advocating a poison ivy salad bar, just use common sense. There are also some cool apps out there that are very useful in the field. I recommend Wild Man Steve Brill's foraging app. Also be on the lookout for my cookbook zine. I hear it's gonna be really good.

Breakfast: Cereal and powdered milk, Pop-Tarts, chia seed pudding, or energy bars. All of these are easy to prepare and make it faster to pack up and get moving. If you don't mind cooking in the morning, oatmeal, Cream of Wheat, or other hot cereals are great options.

Lunch: Dried fruit, protein or energy bars, bagels, nuts, pretzels, chips, jerky, tuna packets, tortillas, cheese, salami, pepperoni, peanut butter packets, chia seed pudding, chocolate, and Pop-Tarts are all good options.

Snacks: Eating snacks throughout the day while riding is important to maintain your energy and motivation level, especially on cold, rainy days, so make sure to keep

One of my favorites—tortilla, cream cheese, apricots, and cashew wrap.
JUSTIN LICHTER

Another favorite—tortilla, Nutella, and potato chip wrap. JUSTIN LICHTER

snacks handy. Protein/energy bars, energy gels or blocks, trail mixes, nuts, dried fruit, chips, pretzels, and chocolate are good choices.

Dinner: If you aren't carrying a stove, a variety of lunch foods work for dinner. You can also soak dehydrated beans and other dehydrated foods to rehydrate them instead of cooking. Carrying a stove or cooking over a fire presents a wider range of options. Ideal choices are caloric-rich foods that have little to no water weight. For ease of preparation consider angel hair pasta, instant rice, ramen noodles, instant soups, instant mashed potatoes, or freeze-dried prepared meals.

If you've ridden hard over the course of the day, you'll find almost anything tastes good at the end of the day in the backcountry!

5.
DEALING WITH TRAILSIDE TROUBLES

The list of things that can potentially go wrong when traveling by bike is daunting, but the reality is you'll likely never have to deal with a majority of the issues that most people

When traveling with a bikepacking or expedition-style tool kit, it's best to separate less-needed items and store them in a separate stuff sack and deeper within frame bags. Keeping common Allen keys and flat tire repair items handy will suffice for most needs.

worry about. A flat tire, torn sidewall, and perhaps a broken chain are among the most common bike issues you're likely to experience, even over a multi-month trip, so a basic repair/tool kit can be kept lightweight and compact. Beyond parts proprietary to your bicycle, you can resolve most issues with a little ingenuity and a bit of help from your surroundings.

A compact repair kit will vary somewhat depending on your bike setup (tubeless tires, mechanical disc brakes, etc.) and whether you are camping, but here are three lightweight repair kit configurations that can take you from across town to around the world with little more than what fits in the palm of your hand.

MINIMALIST BIKE REPAIR KIT

A minimalist tool kit relies on a little luck and the fact that individual tools are lighter, and typically easier to use, than their multi-tool counterparts. Maintaining your bike regularly and ensuring everything is in good working order before departing also allows for a scant repair kit. When carrying minimal supplies, make sure the following is in order before departing on a multiday adventure: clean and well lubricate drivetrain, straighten derailleur hanger, check headset and bottom bracket for play, ensure spokes and all bolts are fully tightened, check tires for proper pressure, tubeless sealant, and integrity, and adjust (and inspect) brakes.

- 1 micro-pump (SKS Sub 40 gram)

- 1 tire lever

- 1 spare tube

- 1 patch kit

- essential Allen keys (4mm, 5mm, 6mm)

- 1 chain tool

- 1 mini screwdriver

BIKEPACKING BIKE REPAIR KIT

Traveling light in the backcountry while remaining self-sufficient takes a little more than a few strategically selected Allen keys, but it doesn't require lugging a toolbox either. With a combination of the items below, you can work your way out of the most common mechanical scenarios while only carrying a small stash of tools and spare parts in your frame bag or seat bag.

- 1 small hand pump capable of easily pumping plus-size and high-volume tires

- 1 tire lever

- 1 or 2 spare tubes

- 2 tire boots

- 1 patch kit

- 1 quick link

- 1 complete multi-tool or individual Allen keys (2mm to 8mm), chain tool, spoke wrench, and mini screwdriver

- 1 razor blade or small compact knife

- 1 spare cleat and mounting bolts

- 1 replacement valve core

- 2 zip ties

- 1 hose clamp (1 inch is a versatile diameter)

- 1 small dose of chain lube (travel contact solution size)

- 1 small section of duct/Gorilla tape wrapped around your pump, lighter, or bottle

- 1 adjustable Velcro or cinch-style strap

EXPEDITION BIKE REPAIR KIT

When traveling by bike for an extended period of time, exploring remote destinations, or pedaling in foreign countries, the likelihood for mechanical failures increases while the resources for resolving the scenario decrease, so it's advisable to pack the repair items below.

- 1 compact convertible hand/foot pump (Lezyne Micro Floor Drive)

- 1 multi-tool or full set of Allen keys (including 8mm and 10mm)

- 1 chain tool

- 2 tire levers

- 2 spare tubes

- 2 patch kits

- 2 quick links

- 4 zip ties

- 3 tire boots

- 1 derailleur hanger

- 1 spare cleat and mounting bolts

- 1 needle and dental floss/heavy-duty thread

- 1 tubeless valve stem and mini tubeless sealant (Stan's 2-ounce)

- 2 sets of spare brake pads

- 2 adjustable Velcro or cinch-style straps

Performing impromptu repairs in distant countries is bound to attract an audience.

- 1 replacement shifter cable

- 1 replacement brake cable

- 2 hose clamps (¾-inch to 1¾-inch)

- 1 Leatherman-style multi-tool with pliers and knife

- 1 mini bottom bracket removal tool

- 1 small cassette removal tool/Hypercracker

- Assortment of spare frame bolts

- 1 small section of duct tape/Gorilla tape/Tenacious Tape

- 1 spare tire

- 1 FiberFix Spoke or spare spokes (and nipples) stored in seat tube (keep in mind you may need three different sizes)

- Chain lube

- Loctite

- 1 tent pole split

TRAILSIDE REPAIRS

While traveling with a pared-down tool kit, you're equipped with the foundation for basic repairs, and as with most items you are carrying, you'll find the essential items can present multiple uses. The following are some seemingly troublesome trailside scenarios that can be resolved without much trouble in even the most remote of locations.

Torn Sidewall

A torn sidewall is an easy fix with a stick-on Park Tools tire boot, but sometimes you're unequipped and other times the tear is beyond what a tire boot can repair. Fortunately, for a basic sidewall tear you'll need little more than a dollar bill or heavy-duty snack wrapper to do the trick. Take a dollar bill and strategically fold it several times to cover the exposed area while leaving plenty of overlap with the surrounding sidewall, before reinserting your tube. The

In the remote reaches of Tajikistan, sewing this cut sidewall with dental floss was the only solution to keep us going. JUSTIN KLINE

reinforced fiber nature of a dollar bill or energy gel–style wrapper will be enough to protect your tube from protruding out of small sidewall tears and holes and keep debris from coming in direct contact with the tube.

When a tire boot doesn't do the trick, or isn't in your repair kit, a cut sidewall can be sewn back together and reliably last for hundreds, if not thousands, of miles. Even if you're without thread, the dental floss you haven't been using on your teeth will do the trick nicely. A heavy-duty needle is crucial for penetrating the thick rubber of your tire.

Take extra care when tying your knot to keep it as small as possible. A protruding knot can rub through your inner tube over time. Using a patch or tire boot between the sewn sidewall and tube can help eliminate the chance of rubbing through the tube.

Broken Shifter

A simple hose clap found at most local hardware stores can really come in handy when you've had a bad crash on the bike or, in this case, when something crashed into my bike during transport.

Being that most bikes are made up primarily of round tubing—frame, fork, seatpost, handlebars—a small assortment of varied diameter hose clamps can be incredibly useful after a crash or incident. Reattaching a

brake lever or shifter to the handlebars, repairing a seat-post clamp, securing a water bottle or anything cage to a fork leg, or securing a rack or other loose luggage to your rear triangle can all be a quick fix with a hose clamp or two.

Broken Spoke

A broken spoke is an uncommon occurrence for most cyclists, particularly those traveling with a minimalist kit or bikepacking load. While you are far less likely to break a spoke compared to those riding with heavily loaded racks and panniers, that doesn't guarantee such fate is completely avoidable. If you aren't prepared by carrying the appropriate length spokes for your wheels, the next best thing is an on-the-spot repair kit such as the FiberFix Spoke. At just 0.5 ounce, this little spoke substitute kit can replace your broken spoke and get your wheel back in true. First you thread the FiberFix replacement spoke into the nipple and loop the cord through the spoke hole at the hub and back through the cam, then use the cam to tighten the Kevlar spoke appropriately.

Sleeping Bag Repair

All sleeping bags will lose a few feathers here and there. Sometimes they're lost at the seams, other times the quills poke through the shell or liner. If this is happening, try to grab the feather through the opposite side of the sleeping bag and pull it back into the bag. The hole should be small and close up after the feather is pulled back inside. If you can't do that, then the feather is destined to come out, but don't worry—a few feathers won't affect the bag's performance. If you're losing feathers because of a rip in the shell material, or even something bigger than a small hole with a protruding feather, you need to fix it as soon as possible. Use Tenacious Tape instead of duct tape when possible. When using Tenacious Tape or duct tape, overlap at least 1 inch on both ends of the rip to prevent the rip from spreading. Also, when using Tenacious Tape for fabric repairs, sleeping bag repairs, and inflatable sleeping pad repairs, it can be useful to cut it with rounded corners to prevent the edges from catching on things and result in a longer-lasting repair.

Inflatable Sleeping Pad Repair

To find a hole or leak in an inflatable pad, submerge the inflated pad in soapy water (or a calm pond if on the trail). Then remove the pad and with the valve closed try to push out the air. The soapsuds should bubble in the area with the leak, and this will tell you where you need to place the patch.

Zipper Repair

Depending on what the problem is will determine if it is easily fixable. If the teeth aren't closing properly, then it is usually a broken slider (unless you see a broken tooth). To get the slider off, use some pliers to cut it off. Once that's done, you can reattach a new slider by sliding it back onto the teeth.

If the teeth are crooked, that will also cause a problem. Take extreme care in trying to straighten the teeth so

Sewing up some holes and glove blowouts during a trip.
JUSTIN LICHTER

you don't break them. If that fails or the thread holding the zipper to the fabric wears off, then you may need to replace the entire zipper. Keep in mind that zippers should be maintained, especially on tents and sleeping bags, since they often get dirt and small particles in the teeth. This "invisible" dirt can damage the teeth and lead to an expensive zipper repair. Use a product like Zip Care on shelters, backpacks, sleeping bags, and frame bags as routine maintenance since they'll usually get grimy.

Shoelace Repair

Some repairs can be easily improvised and resolved by items already in your kit. For instance, if the shoelace or

BOA system on your cycling shoes fails, it can easily be replaced by using the cord from your shelter guylines.

Tent Pole Repair

Tent poles can break in high wind or if bent too far. Most tents come with a little metal sleeve to use if you break a tent pole. You can also purchase these kits separately or pick something up at the hardware store. Place this sleeve, a clamp, or something similar that is a little wider than the tent pole over the broken area and tighten or tape it in place with duct tape. This should help support the broken pole until you can replace it.

6.

BIKEPACKING FOR SPEED AND ENDURANCE

Bikepacking and lightweight off-road bicycle travel is unique in that it's largely been shaped by self-supported endurance races and solo time trial pursuits to cover unimaginable distances in a short amount of time. While many of us are content to enjoy overnight adventures with friends that include countless snack, social, photo, or even beer stops, the drive for competition and pushing personal limits exists among some of us. If taking your riding from overnight bikepacking outings and weeklong journeys to self-supported ultra-endurance events sounds appealing, there are a number of factors to consider when transitioning from self-supported exploration to self-supported endurance racing.

MIND OVER BODY

There is no denying the fitness and endurance component to self-supported endurance racing, but there is an equally, and possibly more important, component that is difficult to train for: the mental element. In our daily lives we are

Dealing with conditions like these can put even the toughest of minds to the test. JUSTIN KLINE

surrounded by comforts and continuous human interaction, whether it be from loved ones, friends, colleagues, or strangers, leaving little alone time in our own head. Long hours in the saddle during a self-supported endurance race leaves little other choice but to contemplate anything and everything—from navigation, nutrition, and fatigue to bike maintenance, shelter for the evening, and oddities that seemingly come up only when the mind and body are in a state of exhaustion. When in such an emotionally vulnerable position, it's not uncommon for the combination of fatigue and solitude to mix up the perfect cocktail of tears of joy or sadness during a competitive endurance event.

When your body is fatigued, a common scenario in self-supported endurance races, difficult sections can seem never ending. Training your mind to remain calm and positive is an important part of the preparation process.
JUSTIN KLINE

Training the body for racing is a fairly straightforward procedure. In some long-distance races, like the Tour Divide, it's actually possible to ride yourself into peak shape during the course of the race. However, preparing your mind for days, weeks, or in some cases months of racing is a concept far outside the comfort zone for most of us. In many cases the best mental preparation is like a vaccine: small doses of exposure. Exposing yourself in advance to the conditions of an extended self-supported competition is the best indicator of how you will react when the race is on the line.

Insight and Inspiration from Ultra-Endurance Athlete Jay Petervary

Jay Petervary has been long-distance racing for over twenty years with a consistent track record of achievements. He is an eight-time Iditarod Trail Invitational race competitor, holding several wins and race records in both the 350- and 1,000-mile bike routes, and has pressed the Tour Divide record all five times he's finished it. Petervary has recently turned his race career into his profession.

At the average speed and duration you're traveling, every bit of weight counts. Where are the easiest places to shave some extra weight off your kit?

Believe it or not, taking a look at the clothes you are packing and the strategy on how you use them. Look at clothing as a system all working together. Also look at the type and real weight of that clothing. Then you can also incorporate that into your sleep system. You can generally get away with a less-rated sleeping bag if you think about wearing your clothes while in it. You don't need extra shorts. Of course they feel good, but you don't need them. Same thing with shoes. I go with the mentality that what I wear at the start is what I will be wearing at the finish. All else is part of that system.

Beyond your kit, learning and paying attention to how much food and water you are carrying for a given section before a resupply is a great way to save weight, but takes experience. I can remember doing my first Tour Divide with a 200-ounce water bladder. Now I roll with three to four water bottles. That's half the amount and half the weight! Food is very similar. I used to end up in a town with lots of extra calories still on my bike; now I try and reach that town with no calories left. Empty water and calories 10 miles before the resupply is perfect.

Are there any items in your kit that are a bit of extra weight, but you just can't do without them?

Probably the electronics—music, phone, cables, cache battery, tracking device. I always carried a music player as a tool to change my attitude or help push through sleep deprivation, but at the start of this I never carried a phone or a tracking device. The sport has advanced, and we now need to carry the tracking device for both proof of doing said route and as an audience-following device. This is all good for the sport. Phone? Well, must be a security thing in this life we live now. Lame. In the winter I carry a thermos as a treat to make something hot. But I don't carry a stove, go figure.

Do you have any tips for someone looking to transition from bikepacking/lightweight touring into the world of self-supported endurance racing?

When you start to race, you will push yourself harder than expected or anticipated. This typically affects the body harder and in a different way than touring. Try and get in some race simulation for several days. Experience what will happen to your body so you are familiar with it. Also know that you can recover and get through these moments while racing. I think the biggest failures happen when someone feels something they haven't felt before and instead of getting through it, which also falls into the mental category, they quit. We take on these challenges to finish, and if it takes longer than expected, that is way better than not finishing at all.

Remember, many longer self-supported endurance races offer no prize money, award ceremony, or present fan base to cheer you on, so the mental motivation has to come from within. It's important not to underestimate the emotional difficulty but instead master it, allowing yourself to push your physical and mental limits. For some, the mental escape from daily realities can actually enhance focus and be the best way to confront problems that are normally pushed aside.

MODIFIED GEAR REQUIREMENTS

While the general premise of ride, sleep, repeat remains the same for lightweight touring and self-supported endurance racing, the gear requirements and packing list can vary, largely due to unnecessary weight being scrutinized when it comes to racing over a long haul. Consider trimming your kit in the following areas to transition your setup from lightweight touring to self-supported endurance racing.

For the majority of three-season events, a stove and any associated cooking items are the first to be eliminated.

When long-distance racing, sleep comes second to riding, so tents can be more compact (or eliminated altogether), sleeping pads can be shorter, and sleeping bags can often be a warmer temperature rating, thus saving additional weight. When you are pushing your body to the limit day in and day out, it never really shuts down into the complete rest cycle you're used to. Rather than dwell on the lack of quality sleep, experienced endurance racers will pack a warmer-rated/lighter bag and appreciate the weight savings right from the start. I've found this to hold true in the

Long-distance self-supported endurance racing requires a precise kit. I've been able to trim it since, but this was my setup for the Tour Divide in 2009. JUSTIN KLINE

northern reaches of the Great Divide Route, allowing me to be sufficiently warm in a 45-degree bag on numerous below-freezing nights during the Tour Divide race.

Besides trimming the cooking and sleeping department, the wardrobe is another area where noticeable bulk can be slimmed in most cases. With little time spent outside of riding, replenishing, and sleeping, there is no need for off-the-bike clothes, shoes, or other attire. If you are equipped for the weather conditions while on the bike, there is little other clothing required.

It's not all about trimming your kit though. Self-supported endurance racing places more emphasis on some items and even adds others to your setup. With so much time in the saddle and so little time to bathe, a proper care kit (wipes, ointment, cream) for your sit region is a necessity. There should also be added emphasis placed on first-aid and repair items to ensure you can tend to unexpected needs in a timely manner. Lights, particularly a setup where the battery can be charged or replaced on the go, is of significant importance since much of the night is spent riding.

Ultimately, the best lightweight race kit is one that provides you with mental comfort and security knowing that (almost) no matter what happens, you've got it covered with what you're carrying. Ask any winner of the Tour Divide, Colorado Trail Race, Iditabike, or other fully committing self-supported endurance race—they may not have been carrying the absolute lightest load possible, but they crossed the finish line first with the kit they assembled.

A quick stop to brush your teeth, and then it's back on your way . . .

The Revolution of Frame Bags with Eric Parsons

Eric Parsons is the owner and founder of Alaska-based Revelate Designs, which has been building bikepacking-specific gear longer than any other manufacturer. Eric has mountain biked for over twenty-five years, long-distance bike toured through Asia and South America, and pioneered fatbiking along Alaska's coastline.

How did you get your start creating frame bags and light-weight carrying solutions?

When I lived in Colorado, I had a friend who flew up to Alaska to compete in the Iditasport races. He had a frame bag on his bike that his mom made to carry gear for the race. I had never seen anything like it and loved the DIY innovation. Fast-forward six years—I'm living in Alaska and seeing the unique needs of winter ultra-bike racers firsthand. I bought a cheap sewing machine and started learning the craft of building my own gear. About a year later I was sick of my real job and was building frame bags late at night and on the weekends. I loved the gratification that came from being able to go from design to prototype within a few hours. I knew that if I devoted all my time to bag making there was a niche market for it. I quit my engineering job, bought an industrial machine, and dove in.

Today's carrying system synonymous with bikepacking derives from self-supported endurance pursuits like Tour Divide. Now that bikepacking bags are being used by a broader, more recreational audience, how has the design and function of bikepacking bags evolved?

Early on, riders using the gear usually knew how to pack and had their gear pared down to the essentials; they just needed the means to carry it. Now, education is a much larger element. Both Revelate and our dealers have to first make sure the customer has realistic expectations for load carrying, as a bikepacking setup is never going to be an equivalent to full racks and panniers. The next step is making sure they understand smart load distribution and how to pack tight so the system works well for them.

How do you see the future of bikepacking and lightweight bicycle travel developing?

I see a boom of creating and sharing of routes. The rise of GPS-enabled smartphones and apps like Gaia GPS are making it so accessible for everyone to create, map, and share their local adventures. This has always been happening by the experienced few, but as more riders get comfortable with both their gear and navigation, it's going to keep growing exponentially. I also see bikepacking growing more among older riders who want to travel lighter, in a similar way that ultralight backpacking has helped people over 60 get out and enjoy longer trips without having to carry heavy loads.

A self-supported racing kit should be trimmed down, but what it should never exclude are items that leave you second-guessing your safety, performance, and relative comfort. The mental boost of knowing you have a micro-puff to sleep warm or a spare set of brake pads for replacing a few weeks into a desolate wet stretch provides a level of mental security far more valuable than counting and cutting every gram to the bare minimum.

THE CLOCK IS ALWAYS TICKING

One of the joys of bikepacking is the many stops along the way, whether to explore, snack, or snap a photo. When the riding turns to racing, however, the luxury of spontaneity disappears in favor of calculated decisions. When multi-thousand-mile races come down to finishes contested by a matter of minutes, it's clear that the clock is always ticking. Having gear organized and accessible while riding can be the difference between winning and losing. Clothing layers, food, and regularly required tools should all have permanent, easily accessible locations, allowing you to adjust body temperature, refuel, and make minor adjustments on the fly.

Being efficient at setting up your sleep system and breaking it down in the morning is another area that adds up time savings. Keeping the handlebar and seat bags on the bike when packing and unpacking simplifies the process and avoids the added steps of removing and remounting daily, which is particularly frustrating with colds hands.

Turning the pedals over for 12 to 18 hours a day requires a significant increase in caloric intake, which

Consuming calories and energy on the go becomes a habit during self-supported endurance events. JUSTIN KLINE

makes eating more than a simple three-meals-a-day commitment. Getting out of the saddle to enjoy some well-deserved nourishment is inevitable, but whenever possible eating and drinking on the go saves notable amounts of time over the course of days or weeks. Sometimes you'll even find that regularly consuming small amounts on the bike is preferable to stopping forward progress and attempting to stomach a large meal. Ultimately, though, your body will give you clear indicators of what, how, and where you should be eating.

RACES TO REMEMBER

If exploring your personal limits on the bike is an appealing proposition, consider some of these self-supported endurance races: Arizona Trail Race, Arrowhead Ultra, Colorado Trail Race, JayP's Fat Pursuit, Iditarod Trail Invitational, Stagecoach 400, Tour Divide, and Transcontinental Race. Many of the routes are also worth considering as a long-distance tour, particularly since most are well documented with plentiful information available for planning.

Whether you're chasing down the Tour Divide record or chasing the sight of your buddy's seat bag along a slice of local singletrack, don't forget to soak it all in and embrace the joy of traveling light by bike. Ride far from it all, enjoy the escape, and strive to do it all over again.

7.
A FEW OF OUR FAVORITES: DESTINATIONS AND SETUPS

There is no denying the allure of a legendary bikepacking destination or one yet to be discovered. Picturesque landscapes, rugged terrain, and pure adventure are what these lust-worthy routes are made of. Below are a few of our handpicked favorites among the iconic long-distance bikepacking routes. They will inspire you to get out and explore more, and there's no better time to start checking them off than now.

GREAT DIVIDE MOUNTAIN BIKE ROUTE

Known as "the longest off-pavement route in the world," the GDMBR is the premier off-road touring route. Established by the Adventure Cycling Association, this diverse routes stretches 2,768 miles from Banff, Alberta, to Antelope Wells, New Mexico, through two Canadian provinces and five states while climbing over 200,000 feet along the way. The riding surface is primarily dirt and gravel roads but varies to also include jeep trails, singletrack, abandoned railroad beds, and some stretches of pavement.

It's an opportunity to pedal in the Lower 48 through what still are fairly remote areas, but the nontechnical nature of the route allows for long distances to be covered, keeping services within reach fairly regularly. The route meanders through the stunning landscapes of tall forests, mountain vistas, alpine meadows, sprawling valleys, and arid desert to give you a truly unique riding experience. Beyond friendly small-town locals, you also have the opportunity to encounter bears, elk, moose, deer, sheep, horses, antelope, eagles, and other often elusive wildlife.

Recommended Setup

From fixed gears to fat bikes, this route has seen tire tracks from a wide variety of bicycles. An ideal, and race proven, setup is a hardtail mountain bike with frame bags for carrying gear. Rigid drop bar hardtails like the Salsa Fargo and Cutthroat were born on this route and prove to be a solid steed for tackling the Divide these days. A carbon fork helps dampen the vibration a bit while keeping things light, but some suspension, both front and rear, can certainly add a bit of comfort to the journey (just make sure it's well maintained and semi-serviceable if it fails along the way).

When to Go

The Great Divide Route has a fairly good window of opportunity for exploring from early summer through fall, but snow in the northern and higher-elevation portions and monsoon season in New Mexico are the most difficult variables to account for. A solid starting date of late June/early July can be ideal to be less exposed to these weather nuances. The Tour Divide race, which encompasses finishing times of roughly two weeks to two months, pushes the limit a bit and departs Banff in mid-June (typically the second Friday of the month). The previous winter's snow levels often dictate an ideal starting date, but often trudging through some of the white stuff is inevitable.

Logistics

Getting to Banff is pretty straightforward, particularly with a simple shuttle ride from nearby Calgary if arriving to the area by plane. The endpoint of Antelope Wells is by comparison more of a no-man's-land, but with a bit of planning, a shuttle can be arranged to airports in El Paso, Texas, or Tucson, Arizona. Adventure Cycling has a helpful shuttle guide outlined within their resources for the route, listed below.

Additional Reading

Adventure Cycling Association: www.adventurecycling .org/routes-and-maps/adventure-cycling-route-network/ great-divide-mountain-bike-route

Bikepacking.com: www.bikepacking.com/routes/great -divide-mountain-bike-route-gdmbr

ANNAPURNA CIRCUIT

Nepal has long been a popular trekking destination for the adventurous, but for the most part has yet to be discovered for bikepacking and expedition touring. The primitive infrastructure of the country, mountainous terrain, and countless dirt roads and trails make it an ideal destination

Welcome to the jungle, just one of the many climate zones you'll pedal through along the way.

for adventure cycling, for those unafraid to explore the far reaches.

The Annapurna Circuit in particular is often referred to as one of the best treks in the world, and for good reason. The route provides up-close-and-personal scenery—but not without earning the view—of Annapurna I–IV, Dhaulagiri, and an impressive number of other Himalayan peaks touted as being among the highest in the world. Today the long-time trekking trail is paralleled, overlapped, and in some cases replaced by a rugged dirt "road." While this has altered the lifestyle for villages along the route (providing better access to amenities and health care) and is viewed as taking away from the experience by hiking purists, the jeep track has opened up the route to be a mountain bike adventure.

Don't let the term "dirt road" turn you off or create an illusion of a nontechnical ride. This rugged path is challenging by 4WD, foot, and particularly by bike. Loose soil, baby head rocks, landslides, rockfall, and steep grades make portions of the jeep trail even more difficult than the singletrack trekking trail itself. Then there is the altitude to consider as well. Topping out at nearly 18,000 feet at the Thorong La Pass, the route requires acclimatization and careful attention to symptoms of high-altitude sickness.

The 200-kilometer (plus or minus 40 kilometers) route is typically completed in two to three weeks by trekkers, depending upon their start and end point. By bike there are

Cruising the suspension bridges on the circuit is nothing short of incredible.

numerous possibilities for completing the route in less than ten days or spending several weeks exploring, by connecting primitive dirt paths to the primary route. At the lower elevations, and when descending the opposite side of the pass, traveling by bike presents a notable speed advantage over trekking. As elevation is gained and the trail steepens, the advantage of a bike becomes less significant. Regardless of duration you can rest assured that the kindness of the Nepalese people, scenery, and difficulty of riding in the Himalayas will leave you with lasting memories.

For those who enjoy traveling especially light, the Annapurna Circuit is an ideal journey. The circuit is sprinkled with guesthouses along the entire route, which makes carrying any form of shelter completely obsolete. Lodging at most of these teahouses and guesthouses is had for

There's no need to carry a shelter on the Annapurna Circuit. The route is dotted with guesthouses along the way.

High alpine snowmelt turns to cascading waterfalls on the lower portions of the route.

a nominal fee as long as you eat your meals within the establishment, which you'll have no problem doing after working up an appetite from a long day in the saddle. Ditch the tent and sleeping pad and just bring along a lightweight sleeping bag (or liner), depending upon when you're attempting the route. The accessibility of lodging and "running water" also means you can potentially pack less clothing. Looking to go even lighter? Because of the nature of Nepal and its trekking history, it's even possible to do the route unloaded with a local guide and porter.

Recommended Setup

There is no denying the ruggedness of the Himalayas, so while the circuit has been completed on cyclocross and (unloaded) touring bikes, a mountain bike is far better suited. Loose rock, erosion, and rudimentary cobblestone sections make the route particularly favorable for 650b (27.5-inch), 29ers, and plus-size tires. Ideally your kit should be packed in frame bags, as the terrain will undoubtedly jostle panniers loose repeatedly, whether you're climbing or descending.

When to Go

The climate of Nepal varies widely based on elevation, but overall it has a notable summer monsoon season (June through August), which makes the fall, September through late November, an ideal time to visit and ride. The spring, March through May, also provides a prime time for visiting

The trail becomes slippery and exposed up high, so attempting the route at the proper time is critical.

the country as the spring bloom begins. The northern reaches of the Annapurna Circuit are somewhat protected from the monsoon by the nature of the Himalayas, so travel outside of the peak season is possible and likely to provide more solitude for those willing to take the chance.

Logistics

Tribhuvan International Airport in Kathmandu is the gateway to adventures in Nepal. Upon arrival you'll quickly develop a feel for the basic infrastructure and adventurous spirit of the country. With an economy largely based on tourism, it's easy to find locals eager to help you with transportation, accommodations, and making arrangements for excursions to the mountains. The current de facto start of

Take advantage of the urban amenities where a haircut, straight-blade shave, and massage can be had for a fraction of the price compared to the United States.

Restaurants and snack shops cater to trekkers along the route, so finding food is seldom an issue.

the Annapurna Circuit, Bessisihar, can be reached directly from Kathmandu by a 7-hour, hair-raising bus ride or, if time permits, can be pedaled by following adventurous dirt routes almost directly out of Kathmandu.

Pokhara, the second-largest city in Nepal, is in close proximity to the end of the Annapurna Circuit and provides another potential starting point for the journey. Its lakeside location is ideal, since it provides tourist amenities and a place to stash unnecessary travel items while out riding.

Exploring the Annapurna region, whether by foot or bike, requires two government-issued permits. One is an entry permit for the Annapurna Conservation Area, and the other is a TIMS (Trekker Information Management System), which retains your identification and emergency contact information in case of an emergency during your backcountry travel. Both are easily obtained for a total of $40 to $45 (depending upon the current exchange rate) at the official office in either Kathmandu or Pokhara, and are checked regularly along the route.

Kathmandu has a dizzying selection of outdoor gear and apparel, as well as a few solid bike shops should you have forgotten anything before hitting the circuit. Keep in mind that much of what is offered there is counterfeit, so evaluate the quality, but there are plenty of bargains to be had.

For connectivity, Wi-Fi is available in most of the "sizable" villages, but don't expect it to be viable beyond checking e-mail and updating social media. You'll likely find many like-minded trekkers anxious to stay connected while gathered by the woodstove in the evening. Local SIM

The 5,416-meter summit of Thorong La Pass is the highest point on the Annapurna Circuit, and a major accomplishment to reach by bike, particularly when traveling self-supported.

cards are readily available and inexpensive in both Kathmandu and Pokhara, but the signal varies on the route and mostly just provides voice access (as opposed to voice and data) in this region.

Maps are readily available in Kathmandu and Pokhara for just a few dollars. Although designed for trekking, the maps go beyond tracing the route and highlight teahouses and other important amenities along the way to help you plan your itinerary. The route is well traveled, so getting lost is seldom an issue, but a good topographic and descriptive map is helpful for choosing whether to navigate the dirt road or trekking trail when the option for both exists.

Additional Reading

Most resourceful information online surrounding the Annapurna Circuit is trekking based, but much of it largely applies to riding the route as well. A simple Google search will yield dozens of relevant results describing the route, typical itineraries, and packages available from the countless tour companies servicing the route.

PAMIR HIGHWAY

If stateside pedaling sounds a bit too tame, and if Nepal is too touristy for you, then enter the Pamir Highway, also known as the M41, in Central Asia. The Pamir Highway is the second-highest international road in the world and tackles numerous 4,000-plus-meter passes as it winds through the Pamirs, often referred to as "the roof of the world." While there is some disagreement over the official start and end point of the Pamir Highway, the core of the route for cycling stretches from the city of Osh, Kyrgyzstan, to the capital city of Dushanbe, Tajikistan. This 1,200-plus-kilometer route is a mix of (rough) pavement, gravel, dirt, and sometimes sand that is the definition of adventure. The urban capital of Bishkek, Kyrgyzstan, is an ideal starting point for the route for most westerners since visas are granted on arrival, and the more difficult-to-obtain Tajikistan visa can be acquired at the embassy within local city limits. Bishkek also provides the opportunity to stock up on food and any forgotten gear (albeit lesser-quality gear) before cranking on the pedals. The city, set among the stunning backdrop of the Ala-Too mountain range, provides an interesting and rare glance into a Soviet-style urban settlement with a less developed infrastructure than you're likely accustomed to.

From there you have the option to shuttle by mini-bus to Osh, or if time permits you can pedal dirt or pavement right out of the city to begin the journey. Along the Pamir

Be prepared to encounter a variety of road and trail conditions in the Wakhan, where landslides, avalanches, sandstorms, and flooding are common occurrences. JUSTIN KLINE

route you'll encounter impressive 4,000-plus-meter passes, barren high-altitude landscapes, stunning high alpine lakes, and welcoming locals who may have little but are beyond kind to offer you everything. The Wahkan Valley, the distant left turn off the M41 after Murgab, is not to be missed. This predominantly dirt route takes you through an incredible valley overlooking Afghanistan for much of the journey. Initially, it is extremely remote, but within two days' riding resumes regular access to guesthouses and basic food supplies.

In addition to the standard route, often a highlight for round-the-world touring cyclists, the Pamir region offers an abundance of remote and rugged auxiliary explorations beyond the main route—high alpine lakes, seemingly untouched peaks, and distant animal paths.

Many westerners have not even heard of Kyrgyzstan or Tajikistan, let alone can identify them on the map, and those who pretend to assume you are referring to Kazakhstan. Not surprisingly, this former Soviet territory is also one of the few places in the world where English is not the

Along the route, you're likely to find the most incredible campsites you've ever encountered.

second language, so it's advisable to brush up on a few key Russian phrases prior to arriving.

The solitude and scenery make the minor inconvenience of the language barrier an afterthought. And if that's not enough to seal the deal, then throw in the fact that you'll be treated to what is likely the most incredible camping spots you'll ever have in your life.

Traveling light through the Pamirs means less suffering on the countless 10,000-plus-foot passes you'll encounter, and also opens up opportunities for even more remote exploration. JUSTIN KLINE

Recommended Setup

The Pamir Highway sees a wide variety of touring setups, primarily heavily loaded round-the-world cyclists who struggle up the high-altitude passes and push their over-loaded, skinny-tire steeds through the difficult dirt and sand sections, sometimes being forced to avoid the Wahkan Corridor altogether.

The ideal equipment for this route is a mountain bike with a high-volume bikepacking setup or expedition touring–style setup. A relatively large-volume carrying capacity is necessary for warm layers, and for rations needed on remote stretches. If this area has one strike against it, it's the food; on the rare occasions that you find something you like, stock up on it.

A minimum tire width of 2.0 inches is advisable for comfort and control on dirt, gravel, primitive pavement, and sometimes snow encountered along the way.

When to Go

The harsh high alpine, cold desert climate of the route provides a limited window for ideal travel. Although winter exploration of the route has been done, the landslides, flooding, sandstorms, and unpredictable snowfall that plague the route in even the ideal months is enough of a challenge for most cyclists without enduring dangerously cold winter temperatures. For these reasons summer provides the best opportunity to explore the route and surrounding mountains with relative comfort.

Logistics

In addition to proper visas for both Kyrgyzstan and Tajikistan, a GBAO permit is required for the Pamir Highway
in order to travel through the Gorno-Badakhshan Autono-
mous Region. Your GBAO permit will be checked and documented at numerous military checkpoints along the Pamir
Highway and can be obtained abroad at Tajik embassies
while procuring your visa, or in Dushanbe.

Note the Karamyk (Kyrgyzstan) to Jirgatol (Tajikistan) border is accessible only to Tajik and Kyrgyz locals.
Despite what conflicting information you might hear along
the way, even from border officers (many of whom speak
little English), do not attempt to utilize this crossing. From
personal experience you will be turned away—yes, even
after offering a proper sum of bribe money.

It's easy to feel small among the expansive landscape in Kyrgyzstan and
Tajikistan.

Additional Reading

Caravanistan: http://caravanistan.com

Pamirs.org: www.pamirs.org/cycling.htm

Beth Puliti: www.bethpuliti.com/tajikistan

For other awe-inspiring bikepacking and lightweight touring destinations stateside, consider some of the following: Adirondack Trail, Arizona Trail, Coconino Loop, Colorado Trail, Grand Loop, Katy Trail, Kokopelli Trail, and Maah Daah Hey Trail. Bikepacking.com and bikepacking.net provide continually growing lists of lust-worthy routes, so be sure to browse or, better yet, forge your own and add to the list.

JUSTIN KLINE

OUR FAVORITE GO-TO BIKEPACKING SETUPS

Every new adventure can be undertaken with a different set of tools, and a bikepacking or ultralight touring setup is no exception. Over the years we've traveled more than 100,000 miles under our own power, using a variety of setups. Below are a few of our favorites that might work well for your next lightweight cycling adventure.

Justin Kline's Round-the-World Rig

Item	✓
While traveling for a consecutive two years internationally by bike, my setup evolved along the way and ultimately ended up here. This setup is ideal for long-distance dirt touring and mixed terrain trips.	
Bike and Carrying System	
Salsa Fargo X-9 with Firestarter carbon fork	
Frame bag — Revelate Designs Ranger	
Seat bag — Revelate Designs Viscacha	
Handlebar bag — Revelate Designs Sweetroll	
(2) Salsa Anything cages and dry bags	
Revelate Designs Gas Tank and Mountain Feedbag	
Osprey Escapist 25 (for transporting laptop and work requirements)	
Sleep System	
Sleeping Bag — Enlightened Equipment Accomplice Quilt (shared) and silk sleeping bag liner	
Sleeping Pad — Thermarest NeoAir	
Shelter — Big Agnes Fly Creek II Platinum	
Clothing	
Base layer — (1) Ibex merino wool T-shirt	
Chamois — (2) Sugoi bib shorts	

Bottoms — (1) casual short	
Socks — (2) Bontrager wool socks, (1) waterproof storm socks	
Underwear — (2) ExOfficio boxer briefs	
Mid-layer — (1) varies by season from casual to button up to a fleece	
Rain jacket — (1) Showers Pass	
Rain pants — (1) eVent full side zip	
Gloves — varies by season from Ibex wool fingerless to Mountain Hardware shell gloves	
Footwear — Bontrager XXX cycling shoes, with flip-flops for off the bike	
Headwear — Bontrager Velocis helmet	
Accessories — wool arm warmers, knee warmers, and sunglasses	
Other — Patagonia long underwear, Montbell UL down pants, Outdoor Research micro-puff down jacket, and beanie hat for high alpine stretches and winter environments	
Food/Water/Cooking	
Cookware — inexpensive/developed countries: N/A; remote countries: MSR Whisperlite Universal, ti cook pot, ti spork, and BiC lighter	
Food — always sourced along the way	
Water carrying — 100-ounce Osprey Reservoir and 20-ounce bike bottle	
Water treatment — (1) SteriPEN Ultra	
Repair and Tool Kit	
Expedition-style repair kit (listed in Chapter 5)	
Necessities and Amenities	
iPhone	
Passport, credit cards, cash	
Small cable lock	
DeLorme inReach SE	
Microsoft Surface tablet (for working remotely)	

Justin Kline's Round-the-World Rig (continued)

Princeton Tec Vizz headlamp	
Toiletries — travel toothbrush, toothpaste, floss, toilet paper, etc.	
Notes	
Utilize a lighter-weight stove when bikepacking domestically, or when canister fuel or denatured alcohol is known to be accessible. Consider a fixed-mount/cradle-style carrying system if traveling long-term, and ditch the backpack.	

Justin Kline's Winter Wonderland Wanderer

This setup is ideal for lightweight winter exploration, ideally on snow. It's also a great setup for mud season and exploring rugged, remote, and rarely traveled terrain during the cold months.

Item	✓
Bike and Carrying System	
Borealis Yampa — set up 1x10 with 100mm rims and 4.8-inch tires	
Seat bag — Revelate Designs Viscacha (large)	
Handlebar bag — Revelate Designs Sweetroll (large)	
Sleep System	
Sleeping bag — Mountain Hardwear Clouds Rest SL	
Sleeping pad — Thermarest NeoAir	
Shelter — Mountain Hardwear Spire 2	
Clothing	
Base layer — (1) Ibex merino wool T-shirt	
Bottoms — (1) EMS softshell pants for riding, (1) Patagonia long underwear, (1) Montbell UL down pants	
Socks — (2) wool socks: (1) normal weight, (1) heavyweight	
Underwear — (1) ExOfficio boxer briefs	

Justin Kline's Winter Wonderland Wanderer
(continued)

Mid-layer — (1) wool jersey	
Jacket — (1) Gore-Tex shell, (1) Mountain Hardwear Phantom down	
Gloves — (1) Outdoor Research liner gloves, (1) Outdoor Research down mittens	
Footwear — (1) Lake winter cycling shoes, (1) Sierra Designs down booties	
Headwear — warm beanie	
Accessories — bar mitts, full-coverage face mask, goggles for windy conditions	
Food/Water/Cooking	
Cookware — Jetboil with hanging kit to cook in tent, ti spork	
Food — Dehydrated meal for dinner, tea, hot chocolate, dried fruits, nuts, peanut butter, chocolate	
Water carrying — (2) 32-ounce Nalgene bottles in insulated coozies	
Repair and Tool Kit	
Bikepacking-style repair kit (listed in Chapter 5)	
Necessities and Amenities	
iPhone, credit card, cash	
DeLorme inReach SE	
Princeton Tec Vizz headlamp	
Toiletries — toothbrush, toothpaste, toilet paper, etc.	
Notes	
Carrying capacity is extremely limited in winter when utilizing a bikepacking setup. When possible use high fill–rated down that can pack to a fraction of its size and fit within your limited carrying capacity.	

Justin Lichter's Sierra Bikepacking Setup

This would also be pretty similar to my go-to gear for a summer trip on the Colorado Trail, Kokopelli Trail, or Great Divide Trail.

Item	✓
Bike and Carrying System	
Salsa El Mariachi 29er	
Frame bag — Oveja Negra Single Compartment	
Seatpost bag — Oveja Negra Large 6–12L	
Handlebar bag — Oveja Negra Loader DryBag Mount with Granite Gear Uberlight Stuff Sack	
Sleep System	
Sleeping bag — Montbell Down Hugger 900 #2	
Sleeping pad — Thermarest NeoAir	
Shelter — Mountain Laurel Designs Cuben Fiber Patrol Tarp and 8 ti stakes	
Polycro ground cloth	
Clothes	
Socks — FITS Medium Hiker	
Jacket — Gore-Tex or similar waterproof breathable shell	
Wind jacket — Montbell Tachyon Anorak	
Insulating jacket (down) — Montbell Ex Light Down Anorak	
Bottoms — Montbell Tachyon Wind Pants plus strap to hold one leg up so it doesn't get caught in derailleur	
Beanie — lightweight Icebreaker merino wool beanie	
Gloves — lightweight Windstopper fleece gloves	
Food/Water/Cooking	
Stuff sack (for food bag) — Granite Gear 12L Air Zippsack (2)	
Cookware — Evernew 0.9L ti pot, Trail Designs stove, spork, fuel, lighter	

Justin Lichter's Sierra Bikepacking Setup (continued)

Water treatment — Aqua Mira or SteriPEN	
Small Platypus bladder for fuel	
Water bladder and backpack	
Accessories and Necessities	
Ditties — headlamp (Princeton Tec Vizz), bike repair kit (see chapter 5), book, maps, trail info, knife, pen, paper, extra batteries and SD card for camera, etc.	
Toiletries — toothbrush, small toothpaste, floss, sunglasses, toilet paper, etc.	
Town necessities — credit card, cell phone and charger, ID, keys (if necessary), and cash	
Camera	
Duct tape	
Cycling Clothes	
Watch — High Gear Axis XT	
Boxers — Icebreaker Everyday boxers with fly	
Socks — FITS Light Hiker	
Shirt — Icebreaker Everyday Long Sleeve Half Zip	
Shorts — 1 casual shorts with zippered pockets (Montbell South Rim)	
Helmet — no preference	
Shoes — Vasque Pendulum II trail running shoes	

Whether you're exploring your backyard or the far reaches of the Earth by bike, don't forget to keep it light and enjoy every pedal stroke of the journey.

INDEX

accessory bags, 44–46
alcohol fuel, 80–81
alcohol stoves, 79–80
Annapurna Circuit
  about, 133–37
  logistics, 139–42
  reading, additional, 142
  setup, recommended,
    137–38
  when to go, 138–39
Aqua Mira, 85

backpacks, 43–44
backyard adventures, 28–30
bags
  accessory, 44–46
  frame, 36–38, 126–27
  handlebar, 38–41
  seat, 42–43
  sleeping, 66–67
base clothing layer, 88–89
bikepacking. *See also* specific
    topics
  defined, 2–3
  future of, 127
  history of, 1–3
  principles, 4–9, 11–12
bikepacking bike repair kits,
    108–9
bike repair kits
  bikepacking, 108–9
  expedition, 109–11
  minimalist, 107–8

bikes, 16–18
Bishkek (Kyrgyzstan), 143
bottom clothing layer, 89–91
breakfast, 104
Buffalo Soldiers, 1–2

calories, 95–96
cameras, 41
campsite selection, 58–62
Canada route. *See* Great
    Divide Mountain Bike
    Route
carrying methods. *See also*
    setups
  about, 31–34
  accessory bags, 44–46
  backpacks, 43–44
  frame bags, 36–38,
    126–27
  handlebar bags, 38–41
  packing gear, 34–35
  seat bags, 42–43
Central Asia route. *See* Pamir
    Highway
chamois, 89–90
chemical water treatment, 85
clothing
  base layer, 88–89
  bottom layer, 89–91
  endurance racing and, 124
  footwear, 93
  insulating layer/mid-layer,
    91–92

outer layer, 92–93
Petervary, Jay, on, 121
planning considerations,
    19–20
@ultraromance on, 50–51
wind layer, 92
coconut oil, 100
competition. *See* endurance
    racing, self-supported
cooking kits, 78–83

dandelions, 102
daylight remaining, determin-
    ing, 63
destinations. *See* routes
dinner, 105
direction, determining, 63–64
distances, determining,
    64–65
double-walled shelters, 74

efficiency, 128–30
elevation gain, 16
endurance racing,
    self-supported
    efficiency, 128–30
    gear requirements,
        123–25, 128
    mental element,
        118–20, 123
    races to consider, 130
    transitioning to, 122
expedition bike repair kits,
    109–11

fabric selection, 50, 90
FiberFix Spoke, 114
fire, 51

first aid, 54–58
food
    about, 95–99
    amount to carry, 121–22
    breakfast, 104
    dinner, 105
    foraging, 100–103
    lunch, 104
    planning considerations, 19
    snacks, 104–5
footwear, 93
foraging, 100–103
fork-mounted carrying systems,
    45–46
frame bags, 36–38, 126–27
future
    of bikepacking, 127
    of creating/sharing routes,
        127

Gantt chart, 24–27
gear. *See also* packing gear;
        specific gear
    about, 65
    clothing kits, 88–95
    cooking kits, 78–83
    endurance racing, 123–25,
        128
    food, 95–105
    list of, 53
    shelter, 73–77
    sleep system, 66–73
    water/water treatment,
        83–88
Great Divide Mountain Bike
    Route
    about, 131–32
    logistics, 133

reading, additional, 133
setup, recommended, 132
when to go, 132–33

handlebar bags, 38–41
headlamps, 35
Himalayas route. *See* Annapurna Circuit
history of bikepacking, 1–3
hygiene, 88

impact, minimizing, 60
inflatable sleeping pad
repair, 115
inline water treatment, 86
insects, 60
insulating layer/mid-layer,
91–92
international considerations,
23–27

Justin Kline's Round-the-World
Rig, 150–52
Justin Kline's Winter Wonder-
land Wanderer, 152–53
Justin Lichter's Sierra Bikepack-
ing Setup, 155–56

Kathmandu (Nepal), 141–42
kits
bike repair, 107–11
clothing, 88–95
cooking, 78–83
trimming, 121–22, 123–25

lamb's-quarter, 101
leather saddles, 90–91
lunch, 104

M41 route. *See* Pamir
Highway
mailing supplies in advance,
22–23
maps, 35
mental element, 118–20, 123
merino wool, 89, 90
minimalist bike repair kits,
107–8
multi-fuel stoves, 82

navigation, 62–65
Nepal route. *See* Annapurna
Circuit
nettles, 101

outer clothing layer, 92–93
overnighters, 28–30
overpacking, avoiding, 4–7

packing gear
about, 34–35
accessory bags, 44–46
backpacks, 43–44
frame bags, 36–38,
126–27
handlebar bags, 38–41
seat bags, 42–43
pads, sleeping, 69–70, 115
Pamir Highway
about, 142–46
logistics, 148
reading, additional, 149
setup, recommended, 147
when to go, 147
Parsons, Eric, 126–27
Petersen, Grant, 28–29
pillows, 70

planning
  about, 13–15
  backyard adventures, 28–30
  bikes, 16–18
  clothing, 19–20
  food, 19
  Gantt chart, 24–27
  international considerations, 23–27
  mailing supplies in advance, 22–23
  resources, 15
  shelter, 20–21
  solo *versus* accompanied journeys, 21–22
  terrain/elevation gain, 16
  30-minute prep plan, 30
  water, 18
  weather, 19
plantains, common, 102
Pokhara (Nepal), 140, 142
Poppi's Power Pauper Trail Goulash, 100–103
pots, 78–79
principles, bikepacking, 4–9, 11–12

quilts, 67–68

racing. *See* endurance racing, self-supported
repairs, trailside. *See also* bike repair kits
  shifters, 113–14
  shoelaces, 116–17
  sidewalls, 112–13
  sleeping bags, 114–15

sleeping pads, inflatable, 115
spokes, 114
tent poles, 117
zippers, 115–16
resources, 15
riding experience, maximizing, 7–8
Round-the-World Rig, Justin Kline's, 150–52
routes
  Annapurna Circuit, 133–42
  future of creating/sharing, 127
  Great Divide Mountain Bike Route, 131–33
  Pamir Highway, 142–49

S240 (sub-24 hour overnight), 28–30
Sawyer filters, 86
seat bags, 42–43
setups. *See also* carrying methods
  Annapurna Circuit, 137–38
  evolution of, 47
  Great Divide Mountain Bike Route, 132
  Justin Kline's Round-the-World Rig, 150–52
  Justin Kline's Winter Wonderland Wanderer, 152–53
  Justin Lichter's Sierra Bikepacking Setup, 155–56
  Pamir Highway, 147
shade, 60

sheep sorrel, 101
shell layer, 92–93
shelter, 20–21, 73–77
shifters, broken, 113–14
shoelace repair, 116–17
sidewalls, torn, 112–13
Sierra Bikepacking Setup,
    Justin Lichter's, 155–56
single-walled shelters, 74
skills list, 53–54
sleeping bag repair, 114–15
sleeping bags, 66–67
sleeping pads, 69–70, 115
sleep system
  endurance racing and,
    123–24
  pillows, 70
  quilts, 67–68
  sleeping bags, 66–67
  sleeping pads, 69–70, 115
  tents, 68, 74–75
  @ultraromance on, 51–52
sleep tips, 70–73
snacks, 104–5
spokes, broken, 114
SteriPEN, 85–86
stoves, 79–80, 82
sub-24 hour overnight (S24O),
    28–30

tarps, 73, 75–77
tarptents, 74
tech, latest, 48–49, 122
Tenacious Tape, 115
tent pole repair, 117
tents, 68, 74–75
terrain, 16

tire/wheel size, 10
touring bikes, 49–50
traveling farther, 9, 11–12
T-shirts, 89

@ultraromance, 48–52,
    100–103
U.S. route. See Great Divide
    Mountain Bike Route
UV water treatment, 85–86

vices, 6

warm, staying, 70–71
warmers, arm and knee (or
    leg), 89
water
  amount to carry, 87,
    121, 122
  chemical treatment, 85
  hygiene and, 88
  inline treatment, 86
  planning considerations, 18
  UV treatment, 85–86
watercress, 101
waterproofing, 35
weather, 19
Wheeler, Benedict, 48–52,
    100–103
wheel size, 10
wind, 60
wind layer, 92
Winter Wonderland
    Wanderer, Justin Kline's,
    152–53

zipper repair, 115–16

ABOUT THE AUTHORS

Justin Lichter has hiked more than 35,000 miles since 2002, including thru-hikes on the Appalachian Trail, International AT, Eastern Continental Trail, Pacific Crest Trail, Pacific Northwest Trail, Continental Divide Trail, and Great Divide Trail, as well as treks in the southern Alps, New Zealand, Africa, Iceland, and the Himalaya Range. He is a "Triple Crowner," having hiked the ECT, PCT, and CDT (more than 10,000 miles) in one year. Check him out at justinlichter.com.

Justin Kline has pedaled loaded bicycles, some lighter than others, tens of thousands of miles through more than two dozen countries. The mountains have always been his calling, and the Alps, Appalachians, Cascades, Dolomites, Himalayas, Pamirs, Pyrenees, Sierras, Tian Shans, and Rockies have all taught him valuable lessons in traveling light. His favorite rides start on the dirt and end under the stars with nothing more than what was carried on his bicycle.